IF YOU DO LOVE OLD MEN

If You Do Love Old Men

by

Virginia Stem Owens

WILLIAM B. EERDMANS PUBLISHING COMPANY
GRAND RAPIDS, MICHIGAN

Copyright © 1990 by Virginia Stem Owens

Published 1990 by Wm. B. Eerdmans Publishing Co.
255 Jefferson Ave. S.E., Grand Rapids, Mich. 49503

Printed in the United States of America

Library of Congress Cataloging-in-Publication Data

Owens, Virginia Stem.
    If you do love old men / by Virginia Stem Owens.
        p.   cm.
    ISBN 0-8028-3677-1
    1. Parents, Aged—United States—Case studies. 2. Aging—United
States—Case studies. 3. Fathers and daughters—United States—Case
studies. I. Title.
HQ1063.6.O94   1990
306.874'2'092—dc20   90-31158
                                                  CIP

TABLE OF CONTENTS

	The House	3
Intrados	Predictions	15
	The Rooms	17
Intrados	A Sense of Time	27
	The Wheel	28
Intrados	Memory	39
	The River	41
Intrados	*Religio Medici*	52
	The Deal	53
Intrados	Achievers	79

	The Deserter	81
Intrados	Patriarchs	92
	The Land	94
Intrados	Economies	107
	The War	109
Intrados	Korsakoff's Psychosis	123
	The Trip	124
Intrados	Lear	135
	The Road	137
Intrados	Late-life Dementia	153
	The Money	155
Intrados	Ecclesiasticus	171
	The Reunion	173
Intrados	The San Nicolas Woman	182
	The Secret	183
Intrados	Casket Price List	199
	The Judgment	200

IF YOU DO LOVE OLD MEN

O heavens,
If you do love old men, if your sweet sway
Allow obedience, if yourselves are old,
Make it your cause; send down, and take my part!

—*King Lear*, II, iv

The House

Time, like an ever-rolling stream,
Bears all its sons away.

—Isaac Watts

I LIVE ON A HILL in a house he built almost forty years ago. The hill will be here long after the house is gone. Both of us know this and take our own kind of comfort in it. The hill has been cleared on three sides for pasture, so that it catches the south breeze in hot weather, which is what we mostly have in East Texas. But there's still enough oak, sweet-gum, hickory, cedar, and pine trees left on the hilltop to shade the house in summer. Along the fenceline grow blackberry brambles and a little plum thicket where mockingbirds start singing right before daybreak.

Originally there was a log cabin on the hill. I don't know how old it was, but I remember it had a cistern and a handpump in the kitchen and that it was pungent with rot when he started the new house. That was in 1952. He made it out of yellow pine he hauled from the sawmill over in San Jacinto County. The house is important because it gathers into one solid human artifact the times, the changes, the decay and loss, in the same

3

way the mind holds memory. And how the human heart bears loss and memory is what this story is all about.

He was almost sixty years old when he started this house, and it wasn't the last one he built either. He liked building more than any of the other jobs he ever had. I used to hang around and watch him work. I liked the turpentine tang of the pale pine shuttling through his hands as he laid the lumber across the sawhorses to measure and mark it with his thick, flat carpenter's pencil. I liked listening to his handsaw sing its rasping two notes—*zee-zing*, high-low—and his hammer whang the nails home, each blow a descending note on a metallic, vibrating scale. I liked hearing him whistle his working songs, "Strawberry Roan" and "My Mother Was a Lady," between his teeth.

He was happy when he was building, not only because he liked the work but because he was his own boss then. He always worked as an independent carpenter, doing all the jobs himself or else with only the help of a few hired men, usually down-on-their-luck relatives or neighbors. He did it all, from foundation to roof. Most of the time, though, people hired him to do small projects—putting in stairs or adding on a room.

I remember my grandfather building the north wing of this house. Since his family had no place else to live, he dismantled the old log cabin a section at a time as he built a part of the new house in its place.

I stayed with him the spring the new house was built. His youngest daughter and I were both twelve years old that spring, our last year to be children. We would race one another across the bare floor joists before the decking went down. The foundation of the house was pier-and-beam, which used to be the common way of building houses in this part of the country because it raised the floor high enough off the ground to allow air to circulate freely underneath. As Sally and I picked our way across the elevated spans, the ground seemed dangerously far below. We had to calculate our stride and rhythm accurately or we'd fall between the joists.

But in that unaccountable way of hills and houses, either

the house has sunk or the hill has grown, and with it the girls. The northeast corner now sits right down on the ground, and termites have digested a good part of it. As for my grandfather, his vision is poor and the strength has gone out of his hands. His fingers are so twisted now, he couldn't hammer a nail straight. I see him almost every day, but I haven't heard him whistle his old songs in a long time. And Sally says she can't remember that spring at all.

HE NEVER drew up a plan for the house before he started building, unless it was a rough pencil sketch on the back of a page torn from the Goolsby Drugstore calendar that always hung beside the kitchen stove. He was not by any stretch of the imagination an old-world craftsman. His carpentry was always from the hip-pocket, catch-as-catch-can, make-do school. He learned it from his father and older brothers on the farm and perfected it during the Depression when he had a large family of his own to shelter. Necessity determined his style. He always built with verve rather than exactitude, and he never had any feeling for finishing work. To him, a ten-penny nail looked as good on the inside as the outside. To do him justice, however, my mother says he once built her and her sister fine rocking chairs, the parts carefully fitted and finished. Nevertheless, what he liked best was seeing a building go up, taking shape. Then he was eager to move on to the next thing.

He built this house in the shape of a T, with all the rooms opening directly into one another and with no hallways—a design called "shotgun" in this part of the country, meaning that you could stand at one end of the house and shoot straight through all the doors right out the other end. Hallways are a waste of space, he's always said. Also, except for the one room where the leg and the arms of the T join, all the rooms have their own doors to the outside. He's always liked to keep an escape route handy.

The rooms are all exactly the same size. Every window is set square in the center of the wall, the way a child draws a house. All the rooms are just alike. There is no discernible reason why one should be a bedroom and another a dining room. The house is a triumph of form over function. Function was never consulted at all. Nor was his wife.

Along the inside edge of the T facing north and west runs a long, covered porch, built some years after the house itself. It has served mainly as a place to stand and watch the rain. In the summer the afternoon sun makes the porch too hot, and in the winter there is nothing to shield it from the north winds. My grandfather's youngest son, still a boy when the porch was added, wrote the date in the soft cement the day the porch slab was poured: "Aug. 29, 1955."

There is a crack running across the north leg of the porch now, caused by the soft, sandy soil under the slab settling over the years. And the son, the one who wrote the date with his finger, has himself settled into the sandy soil in the cemetery in town. He died not much more than a year after he had written that date in the wet cement. He was a young recruit in the Army Medical Corps and was killed when his ambulance went over a cliff in Germany. After the funeral the family sat around in the dining room, hot even in November. I lay on an extra bed set up by a window and cried with my face to the wall. This was the first house touched by death I had ever known. That he was so young, only a few years older than Sally and I, made his death seem to belong to us more than to the older people. I didn't see how they could sit at the table and eat. I wanted to be by myself and cry. But there was never any place to go in this house to be alone. Privacy, at least indoors and among his own children, was something else my grandfather never understood. If you wanted privacy, you went outdoors, into the woods.

The house came down to me through a series of happy defaults. My grandfather, as he always did, eventually moved on and built another house. All my grandfather's children, and their children, wanted the house to stay in the family. All of us had spent at least a part of our summer vacations here. My cousins and I had hunted Easter eggs all over the hill, picked dewberries along the fence rows, popped firecrackers at the Christmas and Fourth-of-July celebrations there, sneaked off to the neighbor's muddy pond, killed snakes and hung them belly up across the barbed wire to make it rain, learned to shoot a rifle. On holidays and at funerals, a dozen or more children moved like a guerilla band among the grownups, who were too busy visiting with one another to be bothered with us.

Everyone, as I say, wanted to keep the place in the family. My parents actually bought it. But no one could afford to live out in the country in an old frame house. They all had livings to make in the city. So for a number of years the house was rented out, but after a while it began to need too many repairs to make it worth the trouble and expense.

Meanwhile, for years and from far away, I had day-dreamed about coming back to this house, of sitting at the kitchen window, one that faces the south pasture, and of writing at the table there. And finally, just as it was getting to be too much trouble to maintain the house, I was able to do just that.

At first my husband and I patched and propped, trying to staunch the wounds inflicted on the house by time and termites. But the kitchen floor listed so badly that the window facings had pulled away from the walls, leaving cracks filled with cottony spiders' nests. Damp and cold seeped through the cracks in winter, and mildew crept up the walls in summer. We tore up the kitchen floor to see if the foundation could be leveled, only to discover that the sills were too rotten to salvage.

So we decided to amputate the east arm of the T and to build in its place a new two-story structure attached to the old house at the shoulder socket where the east arm had been. We did the demolition ourselves, and though it was hard, sweaty work, we took a strange delight in the destruction, as if it were the fulfillment of a secret childhood longing. Children are often excited by the prospect of a flood, for instance. They lie on their backs looking up at the ceiling and imagining what it would be like if the house were turned upside down. I think it's because they want to discover how contexts crack, what would happen *if*.

The contractor gave us helpful instructions. "Just do it backwards from building a house," he told us. "Whatever is what you'd put up last, pull that down first."

I imagine my grandfather still thinks of it as his house, at least the part of the old T that remains. He was proud of it when he built it, though by today's standards it wouldn't pass anybody's codes. It has no subfloor, no insulation. This was not unusual, of course, forty years ago in Texas when butane gas was cheaper than fiberglass. He had lived in many "single-wall" houses in his day, the interior studs left exposed. To build a double-wall house had been progress enough for him then.

"These old houses were built like boxcars," the contractor said before we started. "Solid wood and full-size lumber. They don't even mill lumber like that anymore. Back then a two-by-four was really two inches wide and four inches deep. A hurricane wouldn't move this house."

He was right. The outer walls were hard to bring down. The shiplap siding was only easy to pull loose where it had rotted. Termites had eaten clear up between the studs on the south side. Then ants had come and driven out the termites, caking red mud mounds into the spaces between the studs. Yet even in that riddled state, the walls resisted. In the end, we gave up trying to save much of the lumber and just heaved the walls over whole.

It was June, and the moisture blowing in off the Gulf made the dust and dirt stick to us in a damp coating. By noon our clothes were soaked through with sweat. We would stand in the shade of the hickory tree at the highest point on the hill, letting the breeze dry our damp shirts and skin. We felt peaceful and satisfied. When you're building, you're anxious about doing the job right, but when you're tearing down, you don't have those worries.

After we brought the walls down, the bathtub sat on the exposed plain of the floor with the shower pipes still attached, looking like a small boat with its sail furled, on a wooden platform sea. The contractor hauled the tub away for a horse trough. The floor came up last and easily. The foundation sills, what hadn't already crumbled, we burnt. They were full of termites and rot. It was like burning contaminated clothing.

Finally there was nothing left but the bare dirt. After the sun had shone on it for a couple of days, the musty smell of decay and roaches evaporated. We felt good about it, the way your tongue feels when it searches out the spot where the aching tooth used to be. I wasn't sorry it was gone.

The contractor sprayed the ground with chlordane before he set up his forms for the foundation. I wanted another context for this new structure, a solid slab of concrete for the foundation instead of pier-and-beam. Something termites don't eat.

═══════

WHEN HE BUILT the old house in 1952, most of the materials used in this new structure did not even exist. Wood, local yellow pine, and nails were what the old house was mostly made of. Very little of the new part is wood. The walls, other than the studs, are silver-papered insulation board. The outside is covered with vinyl siding made to look like three-inch lapped boards painted yellow. On the inside, the walls are textured and painted sheetrock. Sandwiched in between the vinyl and gypsum is pink stuffing made from spun fiberglass. The new windows have thermal panes and aluminum casings. There are no wooden facings around them for spiders to hide behind. On the floors upstairs we laid nylon carpeting; downstairs we put vinyl tiles. Even the pipes are made of vinyl. Only the skeleton of the new house—the framing, the rafters, the decking—is made of wood.

I didn't bring my grandfather here to see the new structure going up. It wouldn't have fit his context. He doesn't believe in houses that aren't made of wood. Just like he doesn't believe in insulation, air conditioning, or central heat. He's barely reconciled to indoor plumbing. He wouldn't have known what to make of a house built out of processed chemicals: vinyl, aluminum, fiberglass, nylon.

I feel uneasy about the fake woodgrain siding myself. I miss the good full-size lumber and the resinous smell of pine and the oil-based paints he used. But this is the fetid forest of the Gulf Coast, where the Karankaway Indians used to smear themselves with alligator grease to keep from being sucked dry by mosquitoes. In these pine thickets of East Texas, you have to hack out a place to live on a narrow, unstable strand between growth and decay. What's not rotting under your feet is threatening to choke you with its rank propagation.

Now that I've made my way back here, I've built my own house in my own way. But I've kept a good part of his too, though others have advised me to tear it completely down. I have hopes that the world will outlast what's left of his house. But in a sense, the world, the age, the aeon in which it was built has already disappeared. No one builds houses without insulation and central heat anymore.

And more has changed about the world than just the way we build houses.

———

HE USED TO consider his children his wealth, just as his own father had. During the years when we still got together on this hill every summer for family reunions, for Christmas, for funerals, he took comfort in spreading them out before him like a fan of cards and looking at them as if he held a royal flush. They would sustain him, he thought then, the rest of his life. They would be grateful. They would honor his hard work, the fact that he'd kept them all together through lean and bitter years. They would stay close to him forever.

But at some point the rules of the game changed. The hand he had intended to play disintegrated. It didn't turn out to be worth as much as he had counted on. His children scattered across the country. His wife died. He is left now with, at best, three of a kind, and whoever he's playing with holds all the aces.

He will be ninety-one this year—if he lives to December 28, which at this point he gives every indication of doing. His sight and hearing are failing, and he shuffles along, bent over like a question mark. By the time he makes it across the room, he's run out of breath. But his voice is still strong and his health is good—"considering," as his children always add.

"Considering what?" I want to ask them.

At the same time, they can't help wondering why he bothers. Of course, they don't come right out and say this. What they say is, "I sure don't want to live to be ninety, not if it means being in that shape." And that's not all they're considering either.

Seeing him like this puts a strain on their nerves. When they come to visit he's never the way they remember seeing him last. What they would call his personality (though that word wouldn't be in his vocabulary) has been disintegrating and dissolving over the past few years, like an organism that can no longer keep its cell walls intact. Like a house riddled with termites and rot. The unspoken question that shuttles back and forth between them over the telephone lines is "How much longer?"

He lives about a half a mile down the red clay road from me in another house he only supervised the building of. A narrow fallow field where he once grew watermelons lies between my parents' house and his. My mother has had all the trees and brush that had grown up over the years cleared out so she can see when his light comes on in the morning and when it goes off at night. She takes care of all his chores other than the little bit of cooking and washing up he does, and my father does all his repairs and drives him to town just about every day. He takes a fall every month or so, but his hip never breaks, and the papery skin that peels back from his arm like yellowed translucent vellum heals almost as fast as mine can. Three of his brothers lived past ninety, all of them, just as he is, slowly evaporating out of their skins. So his children factor the genetic odds into their calculations and ask again, "How much longer?"

11

THERE'S ANOTHER REASON I came back here to live in this house. I'd been doing some calculations of my own, and at middle age, I'd caught onto the fact that I'm not going to live forever myself. I began to collect those little booklets about aging—the kind that give you statistics for how many old people there are in America and estimates of how that tribe will increase during the next fifty years. I study the bar graphs and maps, cross-hatched and speckled, that show various facts about the sixty-five-and-older population—their living arrangements, their financial status, their level of education, their racial and ethnic composition.

But the booklets don't answer the questions I'm most interested in. They don't tell me where a person goes when the person he once was isn't there anymore. I don't mean when he dies. I mean when he's disappeared, even though you're looking right at him. They don't say anything about what it's like to outlive your own self.

I have a folder in my filing cabinet labeled "Old Age." I put some of those pamphlets in it, along with articles I clip out of newspapers and magazines and pages I photocopy from books. I even have a series of photographs of my grandfather arranged chronologically so I can see in one sequence the curly hair turn gray and then white, the square shoulders begin to slump and finally to sag, though the eyes are always sharp, even if a little bewildered now behind the cataract glasses. It's a hodgepodge file, hardly scientific. But life, you may have noticed, is at best an inexact science. You don't get to run controlled experiments in a laboratory. You only get one shot at it. And though I know the logical fallacy of the single case, I also know that statistics and graphs alone can't tell me what I want to know. It takes a singular case, a particular case to do that.

When I taught *King Lear* last year, I discovered that some students were sympathetic with Lear's two wicked daughters,

Goneril and Regan. From their point of view, Lear should have retired long before he did. He should have been playing golf on the heath instead of trying to regain his kingdom.

"Times change," a sophomore economics major said, shrugging off the Great Chain of Being with two words. "It's inevitable. He should have bowed out gracefully."

How could I argue with that? It's the way we do things today. I know only one thing more than the sophomore: one of these days, the times will change and I won't. I'll stay where I am and the times will move on. And where will I be then? On some iceberg of memory slowly dissolving beneath my feet, leaving me less and less space to stand?

Death is one thing, I know, and there are ways to live with the knowledge of it. Greek immortality, Buddhist *damyata,* the Christian hope of the Resurrection. But disappearance, dissolution, evaporation? Having no location in the world anymore? Remaining carnal but not incarnated, the body and mind vacant and unrecognizable even to those who have always known you best? Supposing, of course, there is anyone still around who knows you at all. Men must endure their going hence, like Lear, fearing they are not in their perfect mind. Sometimes you go hence, not even knowing what day it is or unable to finish a coherent sentence.

———

MY GRANDFATHER has seven living children. Nine, if you count the two stepdaughters he hasn't heard from since their mother died. Their own calculations mostly have to do with the immediate future. He's still on his own—or at least my mother and father are able to sustain his illusion of independence for the present. But for how much longer? What if his already imperfect mind should get so unreliable that he could no longer live alone in his house across the field from my parents? What then?

He doesn't live in the same world we live in any longer.

13

He can't negotiate its twists and turns. He lives instead in a little self-contained bubble, like that boy in the newspapers who was allergic to so many things he had to be sheltered from contact with the world, as if he were an alien on the planet. My grandfather has to be sheltered from the present. He lives inside a bubble of memory, a fragment of the past broken off and floating, fragile and constantly threatened, in the current of time.

As long as his memory holds out, the bubble won't burst. Knowing this, I try to take in as many of his memories as I can, hoping that the mere repetition may strengthen them. But my efforts will never be enough to keep that world alive. When he dies, it will die with him. Even now his memory is failing. His world is dying before he does. Not all at one time, in one great rush, but bit by bit, before the death of the body. And a body without memory, without a world—what is it?

Meanwhile, I live stretched between his house and mine, between his world of wood and mine of vinyl. I kept a part of his house because I can't let that life go entirely, either. Between his age and mine there is a crack that runs the entire length of human history. He is going to die, and when he is gone, there won't be anyone like him anymore. We build our lives of different materials now.

The only bridge that can span the crack that separates our lives is memory, and human memory is a fragile strand that cannot bear much weight. The past is the most important place in the world to old people, as it will be to us all some day. It's where we'll live; it's home. All of us want to be at home, and home becomes, eventually, not just a place, but a time.

PREDICTIONS

STATISTICIANS CALLED ACTUARIES compute the probability of risks for life insurance companies. Their formula for predicting how many years a person will live is usually based only on three factors: sex, race, and the subject's age at the time the prediction is made.

The longitudinal studies on normal aging conducted since 1955 at the Duke University Center for the Study of Aging and Human Development have been able to add a few more variables to the predictive list, however. Taking a sample of 271 volunteers aged sixty and over from the surrounding Durham community, the researchers determined that cardiovascular disease, cigarette smoking, range of physical functioning, work satisfaction, and something called "happiness ratings" added considerably more precision to predictions made from actuarial life-expectancy tables alone. In fact, these additional categories account for a full 27 percent of the variations that remain after age, sex, and race have been considered.

When these five categories of variables are used, men appear to be even more predictable than women. Accuracy in predicting longevity among men is double that for the whole group. For men over seventy, cardiovascular disease was the single most reliable predictor of the five categories. The second strongest variable for men over seventy was work satisfaction. The psychosocial category was quantified by giving each respondent one point for each of these three statements he agreed with—

I am happy only when I have definite work to do.
I am satisfied with the work I do now.
I do better work now than ever before.

—and one point for each of these three statements he disagreed with:

I can no longer do any kind of useful work.
I have no work to look forward to.
I get badly flustered when I have to hurry with my work.

Geneticists, however, continue to believe that inheritance is the most significant factor in predicting how long someone is likely to live. Also, high altitudes seem to promote longevity. Vilcabamba, a village of 819 in the Andes, has nine citizens certified to be over a hundred years old. Centenarians in the United States average 3 per 100,000.

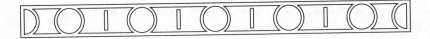

The Rooms

W HEN I WALK into his house tonight, the last house he will ever have, the smell of hovering propane fumes from the space heater meets me, draws me before I know it into other rooms, down a telescoping corridor of rooms, set shotgun style, like all his houses, one memory, one room, opening into another. One lamp burns beside his chair; the rest of the room is in shadows, just as in all those other winter-dark rooms where light was hoarded. The unpainted wood floors are bare. The smells of dust and damp and uncombusted fumes fit around us like well-worn flannel.

After three days of rain, he's glad to have company on this November night. The light falls on his white, thready hair pulled across his waxy scalp and on his long, large nose and ears; strikes his brown eyes, one twisted slightly off center, this his lifelong aggravation and maybe shame; follows the bones of his thin fingers, some of them skewed now by drawing tendons, swelling joints, the hands that he always used to good effect in his peculiar style of patriarchal oratory, moving them not quickly but deliberately, defining planes in the air around him with the authority of Euclid, creating a universe that seemed to defy contradiction.

His television set had been on when I came in. A man in a dark suit was saying something serious about "rock and roll . . ."—the last phrase we heard as he switched the set off.

My grandfather waves his arms at the gray screen from his big black chair. "I don't know nothing about rock and roll," he says, "but I know something about dancing. Young folks'll dance ever chance they get."

He settles back in the cracked Naugahyde and folds his hands across his stomach. "My brother Hoyt and me, we used to take girls out possum-hunting. But if we come up on a wooden bridge, them girls would just insist on us a-dancing."

"Dancing?" I repeat. "On a wooden bridge?"

"Why yes, daughter. Wooden bridges make stout floors for dancing. Better than what some folks had at home. They wasn't many floors could stand up to our dancing. And I usually supplied the music. With my French harp."

"But this was in the dark," I say. "How did you see to dance?"

"By the moonlight," he says. "The moon made it almost bright as day. We could see our shadows, it was that bright."

The tune "Buffalo Gals" occurs to me. *Buffalo gals, won't you come out tonight and dance by the light of the moon.* "So I guess that's what that song's about," I say.

"Of course," he grins, remembering.

"What kind of dancing did you do?"

"Oh, two-step, waltzing, squares. Of course, if you was at some folks' home didn't allow no dancing, then we had what you called play-parties. We played Snap and games like that."

"Snap?"

"Where a boy and a girl gets up there and stands in the middle and some other fellow tries to break in, you see, and take her away from him. But then, if we had music, we could dance. A violin and sometimes a guitar or a mandolin. And if there wasn't any of them, then they'd call on me."

"With your French harp."

"Yep. 'Course, it's all just the same, whether it was a play-party or dancing. Just a chance for boys and girls to get together."

Somehow this leads to my grandmother, the wife he

married in 1919 as a doughboy just come back from the war. And he never mentions her without telling about her death ten years and six children later. It is a story we always get to on wet nights when no one else has come to see him. But at this point I come to the end of this corridor of telescoping rooms. I never knew my grandmother, and I can go no farther. He goes on alone.

She was a pretty woman, judging by the picture of her sitting on his homemade coffee table. The picture is an enlargement of an old photograph one of his daughters had restored. A cloud of auburn hair surrounds her high-cheeked Irish face. One of his brothers married her sister, in whom their Indian blood showed up more than the Irish. My grandmother is a mysterious figure to me. When I ask him what she was like, he always replies that she was a fine woman and that they never had any trouble. My mother, her oldest child, remembers her as loving music and fun. But she admits that her memories are vague. My grandfather's youngest sister, Mayflower—dead now—helped care for her several times in childbirth. She called her high-spirited, hot-tempered, a match for my grandfather.

Whatever she was like, whoever she was, she died after an April blizzard in 1930 out in Amarillo, where my grandfather had taken her and their five children when he got a job with the railroad there, painting boxcars and steam engines. Their sixth child had been born not long after they got there.

"She come in that morning from taking a walk," he recites, "and she said, 'Daddy, I'm sick.'"

"'Well, if you're sick,' I told her, 'get up in the bed and I'll get a doctor.'"

"But after the doctor come and examined her, he took me out onto the porch, and he propped one foot up on the railing. Then he told me, he said, 'Adams, your wife's got pneumonia. And out in this part of the country, that's as good as a death sentence. For folks with pneumonia has got to have oxygen. Now where you come from back in East Texas, they's plenty of oxygen. But out here on these high plains, the air's thinner. They ain't so much oxygen to it. There's rarely one that pulls through pneumonia out here. I just want you to prepare yourself.'

"And three days later she was gone."

I have heard him tell the story a good two dozen times, and it is always basically the same. She always comes in and says, "Daddy, I'm sick." The doctor always comes and takes him outside to give him the bad news. Her death is always caused by the supposedly thin, oxygen-poor air of Amarillo, though the northern plains of Texas are not much more than three thousand feet high. He makes no mention of the six children in ten years or the fact that the youngest was only ten weeks old. Nor that, not yet having recovered from that birth, she was also exhausted from caring for my mother, who had come down with pneumonia.

It has occurred to me to wonder why he recites this story so doggedly. He has a handful of such stories that come up with the same inevitability that a drowned body rises to the surface of the water. This is a ghost that refuses to be laid.

He has no corresponding story for the death, less than a decade ago, of his second wife, the woman I called Granny. That death is a matter of fact, not story. Too many people still living were there and remember how she died in her sleep with her ankles neatly crossed and a sweater fastened across her chest with a safety pin. But my grandmother's story belongs only to him. No one can dispute his word about it now. He is alone in that sick room with her, listening to her rough breathing, knowing that those six children, one of them still a nursing baby, will soon be motherless. Feeling failure, undoubtedly feeling failure. How many times already had they packed up their brood, their dishes and cooking pots, their mattresses and quilts, and set out in search of work?

In 1930 the Depression was just beginning for the rest of the country, yet life in rural Texas had never been anything but poor. Being the youngest of six sons, my grandfather had no land of his own to work. By this time, he was thirty-three and no longer the cocky doughboy returned from foreign parts. He had already done everything from guarding convicts to sharecropping to hauling timber for a sawmill in order to keep his family together.

Yet never mentioning failure, never once confessing any fear or despair. Never. Not even when each move was owing to his own hardheadedness and temper so quick to take offense. How many times have I heard him say, *I told the boss they wadn't nobody going to talk to me thataway. He could just find him another man for that job.* He has never been satisfied working for anyone else, and he never stuck it out as an employee for long.

"I sent a telegram to my mama and daddy back home," he continues, "and a pass for the train. Since I was working on the railroad, they could travel on my pass. Out of all my brothers and sisters, only May come. May and Buck. They was there the next day. And of course my mama and daddy. They come. But she was already gone by then."

My grandmother is buried somewhere out on those high plains. I have never seen her grave. I think one of my aunts has visited it. Sometimes I think that is a room my grandfather is trying to get back into, and he can't quite make it. Perhaps that's why he tells the story so often; he's trying to create it again, not out of nothing but out of a few dim memories and guilt.

He goes on: "Then them Baptist church folks come around. Wanting to bust up my family, split 'em up. 'We'll take good care of them, Mr. Adams. You won't have to worry with them no more.'" He says these lines in a high, affected voice to show the contempt he still harbors for their good intentions. "My children. Divvying 'em up like they was a bunch of damn little cats." He's never forgiven the Baptists for that. "I said, 'No sir. These children belong to me, and I'll take care of them.' And I did.

"May and Buck, they took the baby back with them. I couldn't work and take care of a new baby too. But my job on the railroad played out not long after that anyway."

It was this younger sister Mayflower and her husband who raised the children for the next few years and who always thereafter served as surrogate parents for at least the older girls. My grandfather brought his family back from West Texas and they all lived together on Buck's family's farm, trying to make a crop when the price of cotton had fallen to ten cents a pound, sometimes less.

"Some days Buck'd go out to work—he'd been a butcher up in Dallas, you see, and folks would hire him to butcher their hogs or cows—and he'd come home with a bucket of syrup at the end of the day. You know that black sorghum syrup. And we'd have biscuits and syrup for supper and for breakfast again the next morning."

Now we are getting close to the rooms I know. I've been in some of these rooms myself. It is their smell and their muted light that surrounds us both here tonight. The light from the one fire burning in the November night that, out of necessity, draws a family together.

The fire burns only for him now. His children have all gone away and live in houses with central heat. Where they live, no one needs that one fire. Their children can go to their own rooms and stay warm. Inside the same house they all lead private lives.

One of those remembered rooms I've known was in a farmhouse down along the riverbottom to which no road runs, only ruts made by iron wagon-wheels and once in a while a visiting automobile. The walls, both inside and out, are bare of any paint. A couple of hogs have been killed that day—November, after there's been a cold snap, is the time for killing hogs—and the lights, parts of the lungs, are roasting on coals in the fireplace. The room has no ceiling. Mice run across the rafters high overhead. To us children—my grandfather's youngest three and me—the room seems enormous. The shadows above our heads could reach clear to the heavens for all we know. We are telling ghost stories in a corner, as far from the fireplace as we dare to get.

Bloody Bones on the first step. Leighton draws out the round vowels in his deadest, most menacing voice. *Bloody Bones on the second step.*

Sally and I clutch each other's arms. Her dark eyes glitter.

I am trying to make a picture in my mind of what this Bloody Bones looks like. Is he a skeleton? All the skeletons I've seen have been dry and white and chalky. Even the ones of dead animals we've found in the woods. Why is this one bloody? I picture the carcasses of the hogs killed that day, their steaming guts thundering into the tub as their tight bellies were split open.

Bloody Bones—gotcha! And Leighton's face lunges toward us out of the shadows, his hands grabbing at us like the monster that would drag us down into the cold dark with him. It was sublime terror, the kind that zings through you like an electric charge, bolting you to the floor.

My grandfather reaches from his hide-bottomed chair and pokes at the fire. For a moment the light blazes up, and our faces swim toward one another out of the darkness. The flame-glow licks along our throats and foreheads. We see one another. We are all there after all, and all together.

I like going back to that room, where the terror still thrills and the sudden light leaps up to show us we're still all there, still all together. But Bloody Bones has long since dragged Leighton down into the earth with him, and Sally has shut that door and abandoned the little glittery-eyed girl behind it. I exist on some wild hope, as vague as my picture of Bloody Bones, that somewhere these rooms are kept in an infinitely mansioned heaven.

He, though, ever wary, refuses to be that reckless. Hope has never been his friend, and faith at times his downright enemy. "Don't nobody know what happens after we leave this world," he says now. "Don't let nobody, not even them preachers, tell you no different. What the Almighty decides to do with the world or the next one, either one, that's his own business. He don't ask our permission to run this show. Nossir." Across the pool of light that separates us he fixes me with one of his Pythagorean stares, daring me to dispute what he's just said.

To him, life now is only continual, incomprehensible loss. *Life's full of disappointments*, he's told me often enough. *You better learn that right off the bat and just expect it. They ain't no use in worrying about it. That's just the way it's going to be.*

Just before his last child left home in the late fifties, he built a house with a bomb shelter in it, a cinder-block rectangle sandwiched between the living room and the bedrooms. The bathroom was at one end of this rectangle and the rest of the windowless space ended up being used mostly for storage space, although along the wall he kept a row of gallon jugs filled with water for the ultimate emergency. I asked him about this bomb shelter one day not long ago. He used the word "radiation" in the fifties, but now he falls back on "poison gas," a term more familiar to veterans of World War I.

"I put down these here ventilation pipes in the ground, don't you see, to keep out the poison gas. And then I put me down a layer of sheet metal across that part of the roof and I tarred it—two, three inches of tar on top of that sheet metal. The bathroom was there so's we could get water.

"'Course, they ain't nothing you can do if one of them bombs was to actually fall right on top of you. Won't no bomb shelter nor nothing else save you then. But say it was to hit Houston. You see, there's this poison gas it puts out, and that's what you've got to worry about. Can't see it. Can't smell it. But it's there.

"Now I knowed about that poison gas. I got a shot of it over in France myself. And if any of it was to get on you, like just a little bit on your clothes," he pinches up a piece of his khaki pants to demonstrate, "why, it'd burn a hole clean through, just like a coal of fire. It was that stout. That's what this here bomb shelter was for. To protect you from that poison gas. I told all my children, 'Now when war comes, you make your way back here. No matter where you are, you strike out for here. We'll all be safe here.'"

He may have been planning for future disasters then, but the past is what you've got when you're ninety years old. *Soon it will be just a memory,* we say. *Only a memory,* that most fragile quasi-world, that coarse seine that catches moments, that secondhand storebin of jumbled impressions. *If memory serves me right*, we say. Your cranium is a decanter of aged memories. And even then they may not last your lifetime. They may settle to the bottom of your brain like sediment and you may never be able to stir them up again. It is possible to outlast even your memories. *Life's full of disappointments.*

He is trying to preserve the world by his memory. It is an ark into which he crowds such creatures as he can to save his world from destruction. As saints pray in order to uphold the cosmos, so he remembers in order to preserve the past, his only home now.

And I too like feeling those rooms around me again, familiar, fragrant as threadbare flannel. I too, with this carefully controlled breath, blow a bright bubble till it sags under its own inner weight. The bubble is a story, and the breath that fills it is the life of the past. Within that trembling bubble, moss-hung trees emerge from the riverbottom mists, an oak stands alone in the middle of a plowed field, rain drums on the tin roof, blue northers moan in the chimney, scenes are set by the chiaroscuro of a coal oil lamp. In this setting, everywhere you look there is depth of field, texture, layers of reality, receding mysteries. The past, as Whitman said, is a land latent with unseen existences.

Who is this woman in the photograph they call my grandmother? How did the ten-year-old girl who was not yet my mother survive her loss? Why can't my grandfather stop telling the story? All those faces in the photographs have blown away like scattered leaves. Where to?

What became of them all? None of his children live in those deserted, bare farmhouses along the riverbottoms anymore; they have left behind the poverty, the isolation, the King James Version read doggedly, one chapter at a time, morning and evening. How do *they* remember it? And why is he, once patriarch and powerful, now left alone, his children circling him only warily, coming within the sphere of his influence seldom and then with suspicion? What is the secret running through all these lives?

Why have they deserted their past? Once they reach a certain age, will they too try to return to it through the narrow door of memory? At one point in our lives, we want to be free of the past, to leave it and its limitations behind. But one day we realize we're now the outcome of all our ignorant choices. That's when we want to recover the past. Because if you could get back far enough, you would be innocent of all those ineradicable errors. Everything would still be possible. But by then, it's like entering a second time into your mother's womb.

My grandfather goes back to those rooms, returns again and again, looking for something he lost there. He cannot quite lay his hand on it, cannot remember just what it was he was looking for. He shifts one thing, shoulders aside something else, but it never comes out right. So he goes back again, telling and retelling the stories. Trying to get them right. Trying to get them to come out right, to make some sense. But they always come out the same. His wife dies. He's left alone with six children. He moves on. One by one his children leave him. He waits for another war, for the end of time, when they can all be together again.

But the bomb never falls; the apocalypse never comes. He is still alone. God has cheated him. He insists upon his innocence.

A SENSE OF TIME

LANGUAGE IS NOT the only mental faculty that separates human beings from other animals. A sense of time also divides us from other vertebrates and even other primates. David Premack, a researcher at the University of Pennsylvania, has found that all vertebrates have a "weak sense" of time intervals, being able to discriminate, for example, between sounds lasting for five and ten seconds. Some can distinguish between "a long time ago" and "just now." Chimpanzees even display some consciousness of past and future and are able to indicate by symbols when they are "about to" perform some task. Nevertheless, Premack contends, no other members of the animal kingdom are aware of time in the way humans are.

Premack says that the difference in time-consciousness between chimps and humans is not just quantitative, a matter of holding long spans of time in the memory. Primates other than humans cannot, for instance, "recollect" what being a child at home was like, nor can they compare feelings they experienced in their youth with their current emotional state.

"I don't think it is possible to speak of the human sense of time without including in it the ability to represent yourself to yourself," Premack says. "If we think of the concepts that are presupposed by a sense of our own mortality, one of those concepts would certainly be knowledge of time in the full, human meaning of the word. It is very likely that in all the animal kingdom we are alone in that knowledge."

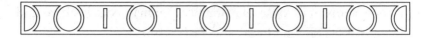

The Wheel

"I WANT THAT WHEEL down off the top of my house," my grandfather said angrily, climbing out of the pickup and slamming the door.

"What are you talking about? What wheel?" my father asked. The two of them had just come back from their daily trip into town. My father takes him in every day to check on his mail at the post office.

The ritual seldom varies. At the post office my grandfather climbs out of the pickup and makes his unsteady way up the sidewalk, studying the faces he passes for one he might know. Inside, he takes out the key to his bank safety-deposit box and tries to make out the number on it.

"Can you read this here number for me?" he asks anyone who happens to be standing there.

"Sir, this isn't a post-office key. This is some other kind of key. Do you have your box key with you?"

"I reckon not," he says.

"Well, if you go around to the counter, the man there'll get your mail for you."

"Will he? Well, thank you. Thank you very much." Then he gets in line at the counter. When it's his turn, he asks the clerk

28

if there's any mail for G. W. Adams. The man goes back behind the partition for a moment and then returns.

"No. Sorry, Mr. Adams. Nothing today."

"Much obliged," my grandfather nods and shuffles back outside and down the sidewalk to where my father is waiting in the pickup with the air conditioner running.

My grandfather doesn't have a post-office box. He gets his mail out on the rural route like the rest of my family. But he carries this key in his pocket, and since it's smaller than his house key, he believes it must belong to a post-office box. The post-office clerk has known my parents for a number of years.

After the post office, they go to Safeway. My father makes the rounds of all five supermarkets in town every week, with his sheaf of coupons for specials. But my grandfather will shop only at Safeway. If they go any place else, he won't even get out of the truck. Safeway, though, he has memorized. He knows where to find the milk and the canned biscuits and the bacon and eggs. That's about all he ever buys, but he buys it every time, particularly the milk. At one point he had nine gallons in his refrigerator, some of them four months old. At the checkout stand he buys a copy of the *National Enquirer*. They have the kind of cash registers at Safeway that call out the prices in a computerized voice. He is convinced, however, that it is the voice of a woman who sits concealed somewhere above the ceiling and who calls out the prices so the checker won't make a mistake.

He hates to have anyone follow him around the store. He takes any effort to assist him as interference. The checkers here know him too, like the clerk at the post office. So my father usually sits outside in the truck, waiting for him. Eventually he appears, leaning on his grocery cart, staring around the parking lot in a bewildered way, trying to remember what kind of vehicle he should be looking for.

They had just come home from the store, each feeling the irritation with the other they always work up on these trips, when my grandfather made his curious demand about the wheel on top of his house.

"You know what wheel I'm talking about. The one up on top of my roof. You ought to know. You're the one that put it up there."

My father, his jaw beginning to clench and unclench, got out of the truck and walked around the house, peering up at the roof. "I don't know what you're talking about," he said. "The only thing I see up there is your TV antenna."

"Well, I don't care what you call it. All I know is I want it down."

"But, Pop, you can't take it down. If you do that, you won't have any TV reception."

"Sure I will. That wheel up there don't have nothing to do with my TV."

"What do you mean? Of course it does. What do you think it's up there for?"

"I don't know why it's up there. That's why I want it down. Can't you understand that?"

My father, defeated by this, went home to consult with my mother.

"Wheel?" she said. "What wheel?"

My father slammed down the grocery sack. "You go talk to him," he said.

But no amount of explanation from anyone could convince my grandfather that what he called the wheel was a television antenna. "I want it off my house," he kept repeating angrily. "Lamar put it up there, and he can take it down. And if he won't do it, then I'll do it myself."

"Now, Daddy, you know you can't be crawling up on top of the house."

"I guess I can. I been crawling up on roofs all my life. And I want that thang off of my house."

So, in the end, my father had to take his big extension ladder down to his father-in-law's house, climb up on the roof, and dismantle the antenna. He and Curtis, Bess's husband, had put the antenna up three years ago. Curtis was dead now. It took my father all afternoon to take the antenna down; it was hot and sweaty up on top of the roof and he kept remembering that Curtis was three years younger than he was.

The next day when he came to take my grandfather to town, the old man was sitting in his chair, obviously out of sorts. "My TV don't work," he said.

My father put the antenna up one more time. He carefully explained, step by step, how each part connected to the next to bring my grandfather his TV picture out of the air. He traced the line from the set up the wall for him. My grandfather nodded.

The next week he said, "I want that wheel off the top of my house."

My father swears it's down for the last time now.

MY GRANDFATHER'S MEMORY, as you can see, is getting steadily worse. He can't remember what day it is or if anyone has been to see him or called on the telephone. That's why I wonder sometimes if it makes any difference if anyone does come to see him. Why should they bother if he can't remember?

Even his stock of stories is draining away. To fill in the blank spaces he can't remember, he's begun to make up new stories. Most of these are about traveling. He claims to have traveled across Canada by train, starting from New York and ending up "somewhere on the West Coast." From there he took a boat. "When we got out there in the middle of the Pacific Ocean," he says, "we just decided to dock over there in China."

He rounds out his travelogue with South America and the Panama Canal. "We finally made it back to Galveston," he says, "and that's where I got off. I was glad to be back home again in Texas." He sits back in his big black chair and stares into the middle distance. It's hard to tell from the look on his face whether he thinks he's fooled you or whether he's trying to fool himself. His daughter Rachel gave him a subscription to *National Geographic* last year, and a stack of the yellow-bordered magazines sits beside his chair. With his television disconnected, the magazine's bright pictures balloon to fill the empty places in his head, the space that memory used to take up.

He makes up other kinds of stories too. The fellow who lives in the trailer across the road shot one of his windows out with a rifle, he says. He keeps his windows and doors shut and locked now, even though it is summer and the temperature is in the upper nineties. When my mother came to change the sheets on his bed, she found a knife under his pillow. His guns—a shotgun, a couple of rifles, and a revolver—are all loaded.

"You ought to take those guns away from him," I warned her, "or at least get rid of the ammunition."

"He'd just buy more," she said. "I tried to get Parker to take the guns home with him last year when he was here. He could just ask to use them a while, say he wanted to go hunting or something. But he didn't do it."

"You know he wouldn't part with those guns anyway, not even if Parker asked for them. He feels like he's got to protect himself now."

Today when I came in he had the .22 rifle standing in the living room beside the space heater. "What are you going to do with that?" I asked him.

"Gonna shoot me a squirrel," he said. "I already shot one last week. You see that big red oak out there?" He points out the front door toward the road. "I seen this little fox squirrel come a-jumping along the road there, and when he got to that red oak he started up it. So I got me my rifle here and I shot him. Then I took him and dressed him out and had him for my supper that night."

That is a story that doesn't come out of *National Geographic*. It's made up partly of memory, partly of hope. He's a boy again, shooting squirrels in the unfenced, open range of Anderson County, not a collapsing tower of twisted bones whose history is leaking away out of its own skull.

He's free. He can go to China, Japan, Peru. Nothing can stop him.

He's desperate.

Last week he told me—this is one of the stories he does remember—about a neighbor of his who committed suicide. It's a story I'd heard several times before, but I decided I'd ask him some questions about it this time.

"We was living in Teague then, and there was a Mr. Harley, I believe his name was, lived sort of catty-cornered acrost from us there. One day a man in a wagon come a-running up in our yard. The team was just a-loping, and he was yelling and carrying on about Mr. Harley being shot.

"Well, I went over there with him, and we found the man there on the front porch. I don't know. Seems like his wife had left him, best as I remember. That musta got to him. Anyhow, he had just set down there on the front porch and taken out his six-shooter—just like the one I got in there—and put it to his head and pulled the trigger. Then he'd just kinda laid back right there on the porch. His feet was still down on the step, just like he'd set down.

"When Dr. Davidson"—(how does he remember the doctor's name?)—"got there, that man Harley was still taking on like a badly butchered hog. You see, he didn't die right off. He had a hole up over this temple here," he points to his own head with his twisted finger, "right above his ear. We picked him up and carried him on inside the house and laid him up on the bed. But it was thirty or forty minutes before that man actually died.

"Before he died, the doctor said to me, 'Adams, they ain't no power on earth can save this man now, for that bullet is lodged somewhere inside his brain. And even if I was to try to take it out, it's already done so much damage that the inside of his brain is all tore up.'

"'Why don't he go ahead and die then?' I asked him.

"'Wellsir. He *cain't* die, not till they get ready for him over there.'

"And I didn't argue with the doctor. See, a man can decide to put a bullet in his brain, but even then he can't die till they're ready for him." He sits back, satisfied with his story.

"What do you think about that?" I ask him. "About somebody putting a bullet in his brain?"

He clears his throat and takes out his big white handkerchief to blow his nose. He isn't stalling to avoid the question. This is part of his rhetorical technique. He figures a lengthy pause before answering a question always adds weight to an opinion.

"Well, daughter, I tell you. Anybody that'd do that, they're not in balance, not in their right mind. And for that reason I don't think they can be held accountable. You see, all sorts of trouble can get to a person. And they can't be accountable in that state."

"You're not in any hurry to go yourself, I take it."

"No sir. I like it just fine right here." He laughs like he has some secret plan up his sleeve.

I pause now myself for effect. "I don't guess there's any easy way of getting out of this world."

"Not none that I know of. Though I *have* seen men killed quick in the war."

"Would you want to go quick?"

"Well now, I don't know as there's any way I'd *like* to go." He laughs again.

"I suspect there's no way around it, though."

"They ain't nobody beat that rap yet. Everbody *must* die, daughter. There's no way outta that one." Then he looked at me solemnly, fixing me in the gaze of his one straight eye.

I took a deep breath and asked my last question. "Are you afraid of dying, Pawpaw?"

He hesitated, but it was not for effect this time. "Certainly," he said. "Anybody who says he's not's a liar."

———

NOT LONG before his ninetieth birthday party last December, but sometime before Christmas, he saw my husband walking along the road in front of his house. He went out on the porch and called to him, "Come on in here. I've got something to show you."

David followed him into his bedroom. "See there?" my grandfather said. He was pointing to a dark blue suit, actually a uniform, with braid on the sleeves and shoulders and a funny-shaped hat with a dusty white plume arching over it.

"Who do you reckon brought that in here?" he said.

David looked at him quizzically. It looked to him like my grandfather's lodge uniform.

"And look here," he went on. He picked up the elaborate sword that goes with the uniform.

"Hmm," David said.

"Somebody snuck in here when I wasn't looking and laid all this out here. A brand-new outfit. Where do you reckon it come from?"

David noticed there was dust on the collar and shoulders because it had been hanging in the closet for years. "Brand new, you say."

"Yes sir. Brand new. Never saw it before in my life." My grandfather rubbed his hands together gleefully. "I just can't imagine who would do such a thing. I thought I heard somebody rustling around in here. And when I come in here later, this is what I found. Now what do you make of that?"

David took a deep breath and shook his head. "Gee, I don't know. It certainly is a mystery."

"A mystery," my grandfather said, clamping down on the phrase. "That's exactly what it is. A mystery."

When David got home, he called my mother.

"He's already shown it to me too," she said. "It's just his old Knights Templar uniform that he hasn't worn in years. I don't know what this is all about. But he told me the same story about someone sneaking into his bedroom to leave it there."

At his birthday party the next week, he told everyone who would listen about the mysterious appearance of the suit. "It just appeared there," he said. Then he laughed. "Somebody must think a right smart of me, bringing me a new suit of clothes like that. Maybe it was Santy Claus."

He sat in his big black Naugahyde chair while thirty or more people percolated through his house—nieces, nephews, great-grandchildren, and others who weren't exactly clear about just what relation they were to him. His birthday is only three days after Christmas, so the little plastic tree his daughter Irene always puts up for him was still glowing dimly in the corner. People he didn't recognize thrust packages wrapped in fancy paper into his hands. Most of the packages turned out to be boxes of candy, so after a while he got tired of undoing the wrapping and merely stacked them in the corner by his chair.

In the kitchen my mother was cutting cake and a great-niece was serving punch. He had bought a turkey for Christmas dinner, but Irene, who had told him she would be there to cook it, hadn't shown up till today, still not very sober. Every time anyone opened the refrigerator door, the odor of spoiled turkey rushed out to mix with the smell of cake and punch.

Outside someone was popping firecrackers. "Somebody's going to get hurt," my mother said distractedly after every explosion. The birthday party had been Irene's idea in the first place. "I'll bring the cake and punch," she had told my mother. "You just see that there's something to serve it in." But not only had the turkey spoiled; she had brought no cake or punch either.

"Go see if Junior is out there with those kids," my mother told me, her hands sticky with icing. "If somebody doesn't watch them, there's going to be a hand blown off. And bring me my camera. I want to get a five-generation picture for the newspaper." She bent down to mop up the punch a three-year-old cousin had just spilled. "It's not everybody who gets to live to see five generations, you know."

"Esther, honey, we've got to go now. We promised Wiley we'd run by to see him this evening at the nursing home. It was good to see your daddy again after all these years. He was so good to us when we were renting that little house from him on

36

Sycamore. I never will forget that house. Nor him either. He's looking real good, honey. Thanks for inviting us."

"Sit down here now, Dad. We're going to take your picture for the newspaper. See? It's going to have five generations in it. You and me and Ginger and Lisa and Seth. That's five, Dad. Did you ever think you'd live to see five generations?"

"Look this way now. Smile. This way, Mr. Adams."

"Do you think there's enough light in here? Maybe we should go out on the porch."

"Has anybody seen my coat? I know I left it in here somewhere."

"I don't want that kind. I want chocolate."

"Smile, Seth. Smile, Daddy."

"Come on, Daddy. Smile real pretty for the camera and I'll give you something good to put in your punch."

"Imagine! Ninety years old. How does it feel, Mr. Adams?"

"Why that ain't nothing. I aim to live to be a hundred."

My mother called me later that evening after all the guests had gone and she and my father had finished cleaning up after the party. "I asked if he wanted anything else to eat, but he said no, he just wanted to sit there and think about the day a while. He seemed real pleased. So I guess it was worth it after all."

———

THE NEXT DAY my father went by to take him to town.

"I ain't a-going," he said angrily.

"Why? What's the matter?"

"Ain't nothing the matter. I just don't want to go."

My father shrugged and went back to the house to report to my mother. "He says he's not going."

"Why not? What's the matter?"

"How would I know? You better go talk to him. Find out what's wrong now."

My mother put on a jacket and crossed the field to his house.

"Dad?"

"Come in."

"Are you feeling all right?"

"Sure I'm all right."

"You didn't want to go to town today?"

"No. I already told you I didn't."

"What's the matter?"

"Ain't nothing the matter. I just don't want to go to town." He pulled out his big white handkerchief from his back pocket and blew his nose into it. Then he carefully folded it and stuck it back in his pocket. "Next year," he said finally, "those people can just find someplace else to have their party. I don't want them coming around here."

"For heaven's sakes, Daddy. It was your birthday they were celebrating. It was your birthday."

He frowned at her. "Where'd you get that idea? I didn't even know half those folks. I never seen 'em before in my life."

MEMORY

PSYCHOLOGISTS NOW DIVIDE the mental capacity for retaining information into "short-term memory" and "long-term memory" because of the very different ways in which the brain performs these functions.

Short-term memory slows down the input of information until it can be permanently stored in the brain. But it can only back up the flow of experience for about fifteen seconds. Then the information must either be shunted into long-term memory or be lost. Also, short-term memory can only handle information chronologically—that is, in the sequence in which events occur. It cannot sort and organize information. However, it can be accessed a good deal more rapidly than long-term memory. It takes only 1/25,000ths of a second to retrieve information from the short-term memory bank. On the other hand, the human short-term memory can hold only seven items at a time; in addition, its contents are easily lost and susceptible to the power surges brought on by shock.

Information passes into the more permanent long-term memory bank by receiving conscious attention or "rehearsing." Long-term memory is always to some extent intentional. Unlike information in the short-term memory bank, information in the long-term memory bank is not stored in simple sequence but is sorted and filed according to one kind or another of meaning system that can also be cross-referenced with other meaning systems. This cross-referencing results in our being able to recall items from long-term memory by "association."

There are at least three subsystems of long-term memory.

"Semantic memory" holds information that can be represented by symbols and for which a temporal context is irrelevant—multiplication tables, for example, or vocabulary or the date of Pearl Harbor. Semantic memory also holds the rules and formulas for manipulating such symbolized information.

"Skill memory" stores information that is also independent of time and space and that is farther from consciousness than semantic memory. How to play the piano, find your way home, and ride a bicycle are all pieces of information stored in the skill memory.

The third category can be called memory for episodes, events, or personal experience. It differs from semantic and skill memory because temporal context is essential to its functioning. One may know, for example, that the United States entered World War I in 1917 without being able to recall when or where or from whom one first learned that piece of information. But one remembers the event of Pearl Harbor itself or the day President Kennedy was shot by recalling where one was and how one heard the news, by recalling an entire episode, a scrap of consciousness, of which the date is only a minor detail.

Whereas semantic memory operates according to similarities within categories, each piece of information stored in episodic memory is necessarily unique and unrepeatable. It is restricted to a particular time and place. Episodic memory gives us our sense of personal identity, something semantic memory has no power to do. Endel Tulving, who researches aspects of memory at the University of Toronto, contends that semantic memory is a "knowing" consciousness while episodic memory is a "self-knowing."

However, since the information in episodic memory comes to us only once, it is the most fragile of all forms of memory, making it extremely vulnerable to loss or change. It is recalled more slowly and with greater difficulty. Each recollection of an event becomes an episode in itself, inevitably altering the original imprint of that information.

The River

WHEN AMERICAN SOLDIERS were demobilized at the end of World War I, they were each given sixty dollars in mustering-out pay. The following year, the American Legion began lobbying Congress for a bonus payment for veterans intended to compensate them for the difference between their military pay and what they could have made in civilian occupations. Since several million Americans had served in this war, Congress found it expedient to pass such a bill in 1922. However, it was vetoed by President Harding.

In 1924 a bonus bill proposing to pay each veteran a dollar a day for his wartime service—$1.25 a day for overseas duty—passed Congress. The bill was again vetoed, this time by President Coolidge. But popular support for a veterans' bonus was so great that Congress overrode his veto, although they deferred payment of the bonus until 1945, twenty-seven years after the Armistice. Veterans were issued bonus certificates to hold until then.

In 1931, early in the Depression, the American Legion demanded immediate payment for these bonus certificates. In May 1932 the Bonus Army, made up of about 15,000 unemployed veterans, came to Washington, where they marched daily to Capitol Hill. On July 28, Douglas MacArthur, then Army

41

Chief of Staff, moved armed troops, cavalry, and tanks to Ana-costia Flats, where the veterans had set up their camp southeast of the capital. He proceeded to burn the camp and disperse the Bonus Army. One veteran was killed. In response to this volatile situation, Representative Wright Patman of Texas introduced a bill to pay the veterans' bonus immediately. Again the bill was vetoed, this time by President Hoover.

In January 1936 Congress again passed a bill to pay off the soldiers' bonus certificates. This time it was President Roosevelt who vetoed the bill. But with one-third of the labor force unemployed in the depths of the Great Depression, popular pressure became so great that the bill passed over his veto.

During World War I, Hoover had been chairman of the American Relief Commission in Europe. Harding, Coolidge, and Roosevelt had all held political office during the war. But none of the four presidents who vetoed the bonus bills had ever seen military service.

———

IT WAS DOWN on the river at Romayor, my aunt Bess begins.

They all say "down on the river" as though they were talking about the Amazon or a legendary country, that far removed from other people's reality.

Daddy was farming on the halves. He never did much farming until after Mother died, although they'd pick cotton sometimes. Our mother, I mean. I think she must have figured she'd already had enough of that. She came from West Texas, where she'd worked on her uncle's cotton farm. She didn't want that kind of life anymore if she could help it.

Things couldn't have been too prosperous then either, you know, even before the Depression. It might have been the Roaring Twenties in the big cities—Houston and Dallas—but out in the country, life was still hard.

Take teeth, for instance. Esther's always had good teeth,

but that was because she was the first baby my mother carried. By the time I came along, I figure her calcium was pretty well depleted. That's why I had to get dentures when I was only thirty years old.

I wasn't even born at home. They'd gone to visit my mother's brother up in Kaufman, close to Dallas. He had a blackland farm there, and Daddy was picking cotton for him. It must have been one of those times, as he says, when he got out of a job. And while they were there, more or less guests in these people's house, I was born.

They always teased me that I was born in a cotton patch. But I wasn't.

There were just eighteen months between your mother and me. Then Helen must have been born in Dallas. She was next, and Daddy was working at the fire department in Dallas then. After her came Rachel. She was born in the little town of Dew, just a wide place in the road, really. And then Ward. He was born in Teague. That's where our grandparents lived. Daddy finally had a boy after four girls. And last of all, Irene out in Amarillo, where Mother died.

What I remember most about our mother was her being so sick when she was pregnant. How she used to throw up every morning. It just tore me up to see her so sick. All those children right in a row—six in ten years. No wonder she died so young. A lot of women did, I guess.

I remember too that she was a fanatical housekeeper. She scrubbed the floors on her hands and knees every day. And we used to go for long walks. I remember that. She liked to walk. Maybe it was because she dipped snuff and she didn't want Daddy to know. She kept one of those big amber snuff jars hidden in the closet. We'd go out walking, and that's when she'd dip her snuff. Daddy never even suspected. After she died and he found that jar in the closet, he never would believe me that it was hers. I told him it was—I didn't figure out it was supposed to be a secret till later—but he never would believe me. "Your mother wouldn't dip snuff," he'd say. And that was the end of it.

I remember when she got sick the ambulance came and took her to the hospital. That was something big then, you know—having an ambulance. Of course, they didn't have antibiotics then, and a lot of people died of pneumonia.

She played the piano. She used to play for church. I don't think she ever took lessons; she just played by ear. Of course, I was only eight when she died, but I remember a lot about her. I remember.

After that, after she died, everything changed. It was the beginning of the Depression, you know, and it wasn't long till Daddy got laid off at the railroad yards. So we came back and lived with Granny and Grandpa at Teague. No—I guess first we lived at Dodge with Aunt May and Uncle Buck. We lived so many places, it's hard to keep them all straight.

Daddy tried to make a crop there at Dodge while Uncle Buck worked out. Uncle Buck had been a butcher up in Dallas, and he'd go around to people's houses and butcher their hogs or cows, and they'd pay him in whatever they had. A bucket of sorghum syrup a lot of the time.

Besides some cotton and corn, Daddy planted five acres of tomatoes. That's a lot of tomatoes. He'd send us out to hoe the tomatoes, and we'd end up having fights, throwing rotten tomatoes at each other out in the field. I can still smell it—that hot sand in the middle of July and those big, juicy tomatoes, sort of sour and sweet smelling at the same time.

Dodge was where the schoolhouse burned down, I remember. But I missed that. I wasn't there to see it because all of us kids took turns staying home to work in the fields, and it was my turn to stay home that day. So I missed the excitement. But we could see the smoke clear out to the house, more than a mile away.

Esther had started to school in Teague, before we went out to Amarillo. She'd come home and we'd play school and she'd teach me what all she'd learned that day, so that the next year, when it was time for me to start, I already knew how to read and write and add. Well, the teacher was afraid I'd cause trouble since I already knew the first-grade work, so she wouldn't let me come that year. Daddy and Mother sent me to stay with another aunt out in the country so I'd be away from it and get over it. They just wanted to get me away from it entirely, even away from Esther teaching me. It liked to killed my soul, I wanted to learn so bad. I still remember that.

I always liked studying and reading. But there never was much time for that, especially after Mother died, when times were so hard.

I guess when we left Dodge was when we moved back up around Teague where Granny and Grandpa still lived, because I remember being there when Grandpa died. That was in 1932, And it wasn't long after Grandpa died that Daddy married my stepmother.

If things had been hard before, they really got bad after that. Grandpa was dead now, and Granny didn't think much of this new wife of Daddy's. For one thing, she was divorced. She had had a husband who just wouldn't make her a living. He'd go off and leave her and her two daughters and she'd have to get by the best that she could. I guess she was desperate for somebody who could take care of her. She had a job sitting up with sick people at night when Daddy met her.

She must have been desperate if she was willing to marry a man with six children already, and her with two of her own. But then, of course, Daddy needed help taking care of his six. Nobody knew then just how it was going to turn out.

Our grandmother never said anything about it, or if she did, we never heard it. Oh, she might have said, Why don't you just stay here and we can manage these children? But that would only have made my daddy more determined to do it his own way, you know.

That's when he took Irene back for good. She had been just three months old when Mother died, and Aunt May had been keeping her ever since. But when we moved away from Dodge, Daddy would go and get her ever so often. Not for long. Just a few weeks or a month maybe. He said he didn't want her forgetting who she belonged to.

But that tore Aunt May up, to keep passing the baby back and forth, never knowing if she was going to get her again or not. You see, her first daughter had died a few years before when she was just about Irene's age, only two or three years old. So Aunt May said this was going to be the end of it. Either she kept Irene and raised her for good, or else Daddy was going to keep her. I've always thought that's the reason Irene turned out the way she did. If he'd only have let Aunt May keep her, none of this would have ever happened with Irene, do you reckon?

It wasn't long after Daddy and my stepmother got married till we knew there was something seriously wrong with her. She'd have these uncontrollable outbursts of temper. Just go to pieces. Sling an iron skillet full of hot grease across the room, or slam my sisters up against the wall, even threaten us with a butcher knife sometimes. And naturally it wasn't but a year or so after they got married that she had a baby. Little Buddy, we called him, though his real name was Medford. Daddy named him after one of his officers in the war.

Anyway, little Buddy was a beautiful baby. Perfectly formed and fair—the only fair one we ever had. All the rest of us were dark. And he was sweet-tempered too. But he had rickets from the start. He never could even hold his head up. We had to carry him around all the time and feed him by hand. He couldn't sit up or anything.

This was when we were living down on the river. We lived in a log house, real close to the riverbank. At night we could hear the alligators bellowing. Daddy had to kill one that crawled up in the cottonfield one day.

Little Buddy lived to be two years old before the rickets finally killed him. He was a big care to us. Somebody had to hold him all the time. And my stepmother, I guess it just about drove her crazy. Or crazier.

Her two daughters had come to live with us at first. They were about Esther's and my age. But they had already left before little Buddy died. They didn't want to live with us anymore. Our life was too hard. We had to work, all of us. Daddy was deter-

mined we were all going to stay together, and that meant that
we had to all work. So they went back to live with their father's
parents. I guess that must have made her feel pretty bad too.

Little Buddy got worse, and my stepmother got worse.
Like I said, she was a violent woman, and we weren't used to
that. She'd throw a tantrum and it'd scare us to death. We'd just
stand and stare at her. And Irene. She was particularly hard on
Irene, who wasn't much more than a baby herself. Maybe because
there was something wrong with her own baby, and here was
Irene, cute and strong and spoiled rotten by Aunt May. And
there we were, the other five of us children, standing around
gaping at her, afraid, and I guess sometimes hating her.

We even caught her—this is terrible—we even caught
her going to throw her baby in the river once. She just couldn't
take it anymore, I guess. We had to take the baby, little Buddy,
away from her. We had to watch her after that. I don't know.
There was something wrong with her.

We buried little Buddy right out there by the river, out
under those trees. I guess it must have been Mr. Dunham, the
man who owned the land we were farming, who paid for the
funeral. Or bought the casket, anyway. He was a good man and
always tried to help Daddy. We put two chairs together there in
the front room and just set the little casket up on them. We didn't
have him embalmed or anything. Daddy dug the grave himself
out under the trees, and we buried him the next day after he
died. And that's all there was to it.

Not long after that the river got up and washed the crop
away. That cotton had been the best Daddy had ever grown. He
had rich riverbottom land, and the cotton was clear up to your
waist and the bolls hanging on it just heavy with cotton. He was
so proud of it.

Then the rains came, and the river started rising. We had
to escape from the house in a boat the neighbors brought. The
river washed away the crop and everything we had.

About that time, my stepmother's father came to live
with us. Can you believe that? He must have been pretty bad off

to come to us. We were so poor and my daddy had so many problems right then.

But then, out of the blue, Daddy's veterans' bonus check came from the government. I don't know what we would have done without that check. It saved us. Daddy paid off Mr. Dunham what he owed him and then he bought all of us four oldest girls musical instruments, ordered them out of the catalogue. Esther got a violin, I had a guitar, Helen got a banjo, and Rachel a mandolin. Rachel still has hers, I think. I remember we had to go out every day under those pine trees down by the river and practice. Daddy was working nights then for Mr. Dunham at his sawmill, so we had to practice outside so we wouldn't disturb him. He sent off for lessons for us through the mail too. We had a good time with that.

Parker was born down there on the river too. We had a midwife to deliver him. A midwife! Can you believe it? But at least there wasn't anything wrong with him.

We must have moved from there to Fostoria. That's where Mr. Dunham's sawmill was. Leighton was born there. At least we were able to have a doctor when he was born. In fact, Daddy named him after that doctor—Leighton Tenny.

Our lives were so hard. I've often wondered why Daddy wasn't more of a religious person. Grandpa was. I've asked Daddy about him, and he says Grandpa was always active in the church. He was even the church clerk. But Daddy himself never did even get baptized until after we came back from Amarillo, after my mother had died. Think of it: a grown man, thirty-six years old, getting baptized for the first time.

But after that, Daddy never did have much more to do with the church. Except for singing. He liked that. Even my stepmother used to sing. When we lived too far back in the woods to get to church, she'd get those hymnbooks of hers out—those old, floppy, dog-eared songbooks with the shaped notes—and sit us all around her and make us sing.

I guess it took for some of us better than it did for others. Ward and Irene, they were the two youngest ones, and neither one of them has anything to do with the church now. They're like Daddy. They like to carry on about all the hypocrites in the church. I'm not saying they're not saved, you understand. I remember when they both were baptized. But they don't think they need anybody but themselves.

What do you reckon makes the difference? Look at Grandpa. Always a deacon in the church. And not one of his sons, six of them, would have anything to do with it.

―――――――

SHE TELLS ME this story while we're sitting out on the end of a pier watching the sun slant away to the west across the lake. As she speaks, her attention darts from one thing to another like the little fish in the water around the pilings.

Together we walk back up the hill to the house she and her husband, a Baptist minister, built for their retirement. He was mowing the lawn before their housewarming party, no more than a few weeks after they'd moved in, when he fell dead in the front yard. That was a year ago. She is a nurse and still works as many hours at the local hospital as Social Security allows.

"Did you ever think when you were living down on the river that you would end up in a comfortable house like this one day?"

"No, I sure didn't." She laughs.

It is a question that people who have lived through hard times in their youth generally like to have people ask them, but this evening the question rings a little hollow. I hear it even as I say it. It's not as though she's ever been well off, though life has never again been as hard as it was during those years on the river before the bonus check came. She struggled through nursing school and then worked to put her husband through college after the war, and later through seminary. Along the way she raised four children and worked with as much ardor in her husband's various Baptist vineyards as he did.

The house she lives in now, their retirement home, is modest, the standard three-bedroom brick ranch-style. Still, she's comfortable. She wouldn't—unless it was for the company—have to go live with her children as a dependent. She can buy gifts for her grandchildren and can afford to travel in a small way.

When people come to visit, she cooks more food than they can possibly eat. She's always done that. She gives gifts impulsively to everyone; she stuffs drawers randomly with clothes, coupons, children's left-behind toys. Life flows through her hands easily, an untidy flood of careless sacrifice.

"Bess is just not happy unless she has somebody to wait on," her sisters complain. "She waited on Curtis hand and foot all those years. And those kids. And now she's back at the hospital."

She asks me now about her father. "Do you reckon he'd come live with me? I could take care of him."

"Of course not. You know he wouldn't. He's not going to leave his own house and go live in someone else's."

She makes no comment but darts to another subject: a mission church being started across the lake, another tributary for her restless energy.

With what feelings does she look back across the abyss of time to that life on the river? She rarely talks about it, not because she's avoiding a painful subject, but just because it never occurs to her to think much about it. She feels none of my grandfather's nostalgia for a lost way of life.

She is not, in fact, oriented toward the past. There seems to be nothing she would like to go back to and pick up again. Not the pale, limp little Buddy, not the tomato patch, not the music under the pine trees or even the lost mother. She is a person who moves on quickly to the next thing. At the hospital she does not like to work with the terminally ill; she prefers the obstetrics ward.

Will she still be like this when she's eighty? Or is there a recursive point, some apogee we all hit in our orbit through life, that will send her spinning back toward that past she has let fall so easily?

My grandfather longs for his own father now. *My poor old daddy*, he often says, shaking his head, although when he was young, he took off for the war without a backward glance. I'm not sure my aunt will long for her father in quite that way, but who can tell? Right now she goes on to the next thing, her hands still open.

But there was a time when he went on to the next thing too—the next farm, the next job—impatiently, fiercely. His hands were open too, from tossing things aside. But now his hands are drawn and twisted, and he is trying to gather it all together again.

RELIGIO MEDICI

SIR THOMAS BROWNE, a seventeenth-century Norwich physician and something of a freethinker for his day, wrote in *Religio Medici* that "the same vice committed at sixteene, is not the same, though it agree in all other circumstances, at forty; but swels and doubles from the circumstance of our age."

I'm not concerned at this point with forty, though, but with ninety. Surely such great age has to be taken into consideration as a mitigating factor in behavior. But Sir Thomas, the even-tempered physician, says no: "Were there any hopes to out-live vice, . . . it were worthy of our knees to implore the dayes of Methusalah. But age doth not rectifie, but incurvate our natures, turning bad dispositions into worser habits, . . . for every day as we grow weaker in age, we grow stronger in sinne."

We all of us bear about in our bodies, he says, like a seed in its husk, what we will be, not just at the height of our powers and self-control, but as we begin our descent earthward and lose our grip on ourselves.

Sir Thomas, however, was no more than thirty when he wrote these words, and at that time had been neither a husband nor a father.

The Deal

I have heard him oft maintain it to be fit, that, sons at perfect age, and fathers declining, the father should be as ward to the son, and the son manage his revenue.

—*King Lear*, I, ii

"ESTHER? Is that you?" His voice sounded more agitated than usual on the phone.

"Yes, Daddy. What is it? Is anything wrong?"

"I want you to come down here."

"I'll be there in a minute."

She noticed her hands were shaking as she wrapped a scarf around her ears. It was misting rain outside. She could feel her heart throbbing in her throat as though she were a child again. What was wrong now?

He was standing on his back porch, pointing out toward his back lot as she came up the steps. "Look at that," he said. "Someone's ruined my peach tree."

She turned and squinted through the mist. "I can't see what you're talking about, Daddy."

"Come on here, then. I'll show you." He took her by the arm, guiding her as though she were a guilty child being led to the scene of her crime, despite the fact that he had to lean on her to get down the steps. He stumped through the damp sand down a row of peach trees to the last one nearest the woods. The bark was stripped off one side of the young tree, and a branch was hanging broken.

"Somebody's ruined my peach tree," he repeated.

"It could have been a deer, you know, Daddy. They strip the bark off trees like that sometimes."

"That ain't no deer," he said, turning back to the house. "It was a human done that. There's someone in this neighborhood did that, someone that's out to get me."

She followed him up the steps and into the house, her heart beating against the sides of her throat and her mouth dry.

"Now Daddy, you know there's no one around here out to get you. That's foolish."

"I know there is too done it. They're a-trying to do me harm."

"Well, who do you think did it, then? Was it me? Was it Lamar? Was it some of the kids?"

"I know you didn't do it," he said pointedly. "But some human did it. Someone that's out to get to me, that don't want me here."

"And just who would that be?"

"How would I know?" he said angrily—then, looking at her out of the corner of his eye, "Lamar was around here yesterday, wasn't he?"

She sat down on the couch and clenched her fists together on her knees. She could feel the blood pounding against her eardrums now, and her eyes were stinging. "Just what do you mean by that? Surely you don't believe Lamar would do something like that."

"What did I say? Did I accuse anyone? All I said was he's been around here."

"But Lamar—"

"Some human ruined that peach tree, I'm telling you."
He was still standing.

"No one's trying to do you any harm, Dad. That's ridiculous. Why would anybody be out to get you?"

"How would I know? But I'm not going to put up with it." He was shaking with fury. "I never have, and I'm not going to start now."

"No, you always made a point of telling people off, people you imagined were out to get you. And you never cared what that meant for anybody else."

"What do you mean by that?"

"That's why I ended up going to sixteen different schools in eleven years. All you cared about was your pride being injured. 'I don't need nothing from nobody,' you always said." She mimicked his petulant voice.

"I never did, neither. I made my own way in the world." He was breathing hard. "And I'll tell you something else, lady. I never wanted to come here to live in the first place. This here was your idea. You know I wanted to go down on the river."

"And just who would have looked after you then, I'd like to know?" She spoke through tears now. "Nothing would do you till you got this house built and the land cleared so you could plant a garden."

"And look at it now! Someone tearing up my fruit trees! But I'm going to get 'em, I can tell you. They come over here messing around, and I'm likely to shoot 'em. I got me a gun right in there, and I'll sure use it on anyone comes messing around my place."

"You better watch out who you're shooting. You might be shooting one of your own children. The last time Parker came to see you and got here after dark, he was afraid to even come to the door because he knows how you brag about your guns, and he didn't want you shooting him by mistake."

"I wouldn't shoot one of my own children and you know it."

"How would you know?" She had stopped crying. "You'd

be so concerned about shooting you wouldn't even know who it was. You better find out who it is you're aiming at before you pull that trigger."

They came to a pause, and both of them sat there panting a bit, casting about for their next gambit. She took a deep breath and tried to pitch her voice in a conciliatory tone.

"Surely you don't think Lamar damaged your peach tree, Dad."

"Well, who else could it a been?"

"No. You can't think that." She stared up at him, dizzy with disbelief, wondering who this person was. Was he sick? Was he crazy? Or was this the way he'd always been, secretly bitter and full of rage? Was this the final fruit of his life?

"Not one of you kids—not one of you—could wait to get away from home. After I'd put you through school and everthing. After you'd gotten all you wanted out of me."

"Daddy. What do you mean? What are you talking about?"

"You know what I mean. I sold a cow out there in Dayton, after you'd graduated from high school, so's I could send you to business school. Nothing would do you but to go to Houston to that business school. And you never came back. Not one of you ever came back."

"But Dad. You remember how it was," she said in an astonished voice. "We grew up. We had to get jobs."

"You never paid me back for that cow neither."

"But Dad, you said that I was to help the next one after I got a job, and then that one would help the next one, and so on. That's what you told me when you sold that cow."

"So?"

"So I helped Bess go to nursing school. And after she and Curtis got married and they were out in Brownwood going to college, Lamar and I sent them fifty dollars every month as long as they were in school."

"Well, I didn't know about that."

"There's a lot you don't know about." She stood up, wanting to leave now, to calm down.

But as she put her hand on the doorknob, he said, "You're not my only child, you know. You just like to act like you're number one. But I can take care of my own business. I don't have to live here."

She turned back. His thready white hair stood out stiffly from his shiny scalp, and the rims of his eyelids were red. "And just where do you think you'd go?" she asked.

"I could go to Conroe. I could go anywhere I please. I could go to the Masonic Home."

"All right, Dad. Why don't you just think about that awhile." She opened the door now, determined to escape this time.

He followed her to the door and stood there as she went down the porch steps into the misty rain. "I'm going to sell this place!" he called after her.

She walked on down the road in the rain, not turning back toward her own house. At the bottom of the hill is a dirty little creek where the trailer across the road empties its waste water. Years ago my grandfather helped the county build a bridge across the creek, a wooden bridge, the heavy pilings soaked in creosote so that on hot summer days it smelled like pitch. Children used to sit and dangle their feet over the side, staring down into the water below, trying to see the frogs and turtles and snakes that lived there.

The old bridge was high up over the water—at least it seemed that way to children—and it rumbled when you crossed it in a car. But several years ago the county filled in the draw and replaced the bridge with a steel culvert. The culvert made the stream more like a ditch. People from town—mostly college students at the end of the term—sometimes dump their trash there now. But it doesn't stay around forever. The next big rain, maybe a hurricane reaching in from the Gulf, washes it away into Locke's pond, like cleaning out a dirty drain.

Still, all that debris must end up someplace, she figured. How much garbage must have collected over the years on the bottom of the pond? Years ago it would have been the kind of garbage that would have dissolved there in the mud eventually—paper, tin cans, even cotton mattresses. But now there was aluminum and Styrofoam. She didn't suppose they would ever dissolve.

And what was at the bottom of her father? That's what she wanted to know. He seemed as murky as the pond to her now. What had happened to his generosity, his honesty, his fidelity? Was indissoluble refuse filling him up? Hard nuggets of resentment, fear, stinginess? That couldn't be. That couldn't happen. All the good things about a person couldn't just disappear, dissolve. But why did he say such cruel things then?

Instead of turning around at the bottom of the hill, she went on up the road. She didn't want Lamar to see her like this.

"Maybe this is just the Lord's way of preparing me," she told me when she got to my house. "Maybe he's just getting me ready to give Daddy up."

"That could be."

"I don't know what to do. I don't know what else I can do."

"You're doing all you can, Mother."

"Remember that time we took him to the Masonic Home in Arlington?"

"Sure."

"It's such a nice place. Clean. Not like some of those awful places. And he'd have somebody to talk to. He wouldn't be so lonely."

"I know."

There was a pause, and I knew she wanted me to carry the burden of the conversation for a while. We have to go through the entire cycle of this antiphon ever so often. It's the only way she can get any relief, even for a little while. "It was very nice under the big trees out in that pecan grove. Lots of space. How many acres did you say it was?"

58

"Oh, over three hundred, I believe they said."

"Plenty of space, even in the city there. That's where we had the picnic. Set up under the trees."

"We took him through all the buildings so he could see," she recited. "Nice rooms. Their own rooms. They can bring their own furniture if they want. Have TV in their own rooms. There was a nice dining room. Good meals."

"Rockers on the front porch of that one building. Remember?"

"Yes. Then it started raining, and we had to get in the car."

"And that's when I asked him, 'Pawpaw, how do you like this place?' And he said, 'Wellsir, I'm mighty proud that these old folks have such a fine place to live and people to look after them.'"

"And that's when we knew he wasn't intending to go there."

"No. Now if he and Granny had gone ahead when she was still alive . . ."

"Yes. But when he found out you had to give them the deed to your property and all that you had in the bank . . ."

"No. He wasn't about to do that. Not that it wouldn't be worth it. But even if he did go, knowing him, there'd be nothing to stop him from getting mad and just walking away from the place the next day. That's what would happen. I just know it."

"Well, you tried, Mother. You've done everything you know how to do."

She put her head down on the table. "I can't stand it. I just can't stand it," she said. I reached over and patted her shoulder. She straightened up and pulled a Kleenex out of her pocket.

"What am I going to do if he tries to sell the place?"

I shrugged. "I wouldn't worry about it. Surely you don't think he's capable of pulling off something like that in his shape."

She bit her bottom lip. "I don't know what to do. I just don't know what else to do."

She blew her nose, took a deep breath, and pitched her voice in a lower tone, the way somebody does to let you know they're all right. "He came to see me once when I was at that business school in Houston. It was so hard. I was living with Tom and Ruby, my cousins. That's the only way I could afford to go. Selling that cow had just provided the tuition money. I had to ride the bus downtown everyday and home again at night if Tom forgot to pick me up. I never had even been on a big city bus before. I was so afraid. Everybody else seemed to know everything—how to dress and talk and get around. Most of the people knew somebody else in the school, but I didn't know anybody. I didn't have a single friend in that whole city. And I was so scared I didn't know how to make any friends. I was just a gawky country girl, and so poor I didn't even have an extra nickel to spend on a Coke. Tom and Ruby were good to me, but they were used to the city. They didn't know how I felt. So far from home." She squeezed the Kleenex up into a tight ball.

"One day when I was sitting in class, I looked up, and there was Daddy. He'd come to see me. He had on his old work khakis like he always wears. I mean, they were clean and everything, but it was still obvious he was a farmer from the country. I was so excited to see him! I was so proud that he'd come. After class he asked me if he had embarrassed me, coming like that, not dressed up or anything. 'You couldn't ever embarrass me, Daddy,' I told him. He was so fine, so brave in all his troubles. He's always kept right on, no matter what. I was proud of him, Gin, I was proud. And so happy he'd come to see me."

She laid her head down on the table again. "Dear God," she said. "I hope I don't ever live long enough to say such hurtful things to you."

"Don't worry, Mother. Don't worry. He doesn't know what he's saying."

"But he must mean it. How else could he have carried that around all those years, about that cow he sold, if he didn't begrudge it? All these years he thinks I've been ungrateful. How *could* he? I don't see what else I could have done."

"You could have stayed home with him for the rest of your life," I said impatiently. "You could have never changed. You could have kept him from changing. You could have made time stand still."

She raised her head and frowned at me. "What are you talking about?"

"That's what he wants, isn't it? Isn't that what he really wants? Never to get old, never to die. Never to have his children leave home or anyone leave him?"

She shook her head and sighed. "I don't know what he wants. Sometimes I think I don't even know who he is anymore. The doctor told me to remember that it's not really him talking. But if it's not him, Gin, then who is it?"

━━━━━━

I WAS WRONG. I had thought that it would be impossible for someone who was nearly blind, as deaf as a post, and unfamiliar with modern marketing to sell a house on his own. It turned out to be less trouble than even he had imagined.

For one thing, it's not unusual for a car to pull alongside me as I'm walking back and forth between my house and my grandfather's and for the driver to ask me if there's any place for sale around here. Sometimes it's a family with children in the backseat, dreaming about a place in the country. Sometimes it's a developer looking for acreage to subdivide. A pizza king once tried to buy our place on the hill. He owns a horse farm right behind us and wanted the old house for his Mexican laborers.

I must admit it's gratifying when somebody wants to buy something you don't have to sell, when you can afford to smile and allow as how, so far as you know, you and all your neighbors are content to stay put right where you are. Sorry. And you wave as they pull away.

Except my grandfather wasn't content. This, of course, was no change for him. He's been restless all his life. And I suppose restlessness and discontent must generate certain airborne signals, like pheromones, that stimulate a response in anyone who thinks he can fix that discontent. In this case it was Rayford Renfro.

Rayford worked at The Walls in Huntsville, the main prison for the Texas Department of Corrections. Over the years he'd worked himself up to a supervisory position, and, since his two children (Wyvonne and Dwayne) had both recently passed their eighteenth birthdays, he no longer had to make monthly child-support payments to his ex-wife, Coreen. Finding himself in this unusually solvent position, Rayford figured that the thing to do, rather than letting that extra money get away from him, was to invest it. After all, he had his retirement coming up in a few more years. So instead of buying himself a new bass boat, he thought he'd put the money into some rental property. Some little frame house, outside of town so he wouldn't have to pay city taxes on it, but close enough to town so he could rent it to college students. You could make more off of college students than colored folks, the man who runs the furniture department at Montgomery Ward's had told him.

So one sunny March day, when my grandfather's restless pheromones must have been particularly active and the wind was up enough to carry them a good distance, Rayford came bumping along our red clay road, across the culvert, and up the sand hill to my grandfather's house. The Milgrams' brick house on the right side of the road and my parents' brick house at the end of the road were both obviously not for sale, nor were they the kind of property that Rayford had his eye out for. However, Ben Milgram's younger brother Pat, whom we all suspect of dealing drugs, lives in the trailer on the unmowed acre next to Ben's house. Since the trailer's front screen is off the hinges and an old washing machine sits out in front among the weeds, this looked like it might be Rayford Renfro's kind of place.

Then he spotted my grandfather's white frame house—just what he'd been hoping for. A propane tank sat beside the well housing. Five rosebushes, badly in need of pruning, lined the weedy ditch in front of the house. And it had two front doors. He pulled into the driveway, noting the white caliche rock that had been hauled in for a base, and got out of his pickup. He had a Camaro at home too, but he knew better than to drive it when he went on his property-hunting excursions in the country.

I don't know that my grandfather can actually hear when anybody comes up on the front porch, but he can feel the house tremble slightly, especially when the person walking across the porch weighs as much as Rayford and is wearing cowboy boots with roper heels. He was already at the front screen door by the time Rayford reached it.

"Yessir? What can I do for you?" He kept his hand on the screen latch.

"Afternoon," Rayford said. "Name's Rayford J. Renfro." He stood on the other side of the screen and planted his hands on his hips as he swung his head slowly around, surveying the property. "Nice place you got here."

"Built it myself," my grandfather said, forgetting that he hadn't.

"That so? Lived here long?"

My grandfather took his hand off the latch and moved back from the door a half-step. "Good little bit," he replied warily. He's suspicious of questions from strangers. He believes they might be agents from the VA, trying to take his benefits away from him. "What was it that you were a-looking for?"

"Well, I tell you, sir. I'm looking to buy me a place out in the country, away from town. You know what I mean?" His survey completed, he turned his attention back to my grandfather and took his hat off.

"That so?"

"Yep, I've had enough of living in town. I mean, the crime and all. It gets to a person after a while."

My grandfather said nothing to this, only blinked through his cataract glasses at Rayford, who was using up his opening gambits rapidly.

"Anyway, what I was wondering was, do you know anybody hereabouts who might have some place to sell? Just a little place is all I'd need. Oh, say, about an acre or so. So's I could grow me some sweet corn, maybe, and some watermelons."

"This sand hill right here grows the best watermelons you'll ever see. Why don't you come in, Mr.—what did you say your name was?"

And thus, whether brought together by scent spores or the stars, my grandfather and Rayford Renfro began to concoct a bargain. Actually, the bargain was practically all on Rayford's side. It took him only about five minutes of shouting into my grandfather's deaf ear to realize it would be child's play to disengage the old man from his house, one perfectly adapted, with its two bedrooms and a bath on each side, for students. He figured he could make at least three hundred dollars a month from it. If the old guy wouldn't go too high on the price, he might even be able to get the bass boat too.

"You ever thought about selling your place here?" he shouted, leaning across the lamp table that separates the two big chairs and trying not to knock off any of the accumulated National Geographics, Masonic books, dusty corn pads, or harmonicas stacked on it.

"Son," my grandfather laughed and pinched up the creases in his khakis between his bent fingers, "ever thang I've got's for sale. Anybody wants to give me the right price for it."

"How much you take for this place, do you reckon?" Rayford began to sweat at this point, even though it was only March. He was beginning to realize that 1930 was as yesterday to this old man. His idea of prices might be as much a part of the past as his watermelons.

My grandfather cleared his throat and looked solemn. "Well, I don't rightly know. How much you think it's worth?"

Rayford pointedly eyed the unfinished flooring and the place on the wall where the soot from the space heater collected. "Hard to say. I'd have to look it over some. Seems like it might need a little fixing up."

"Fixing up? Why, boy, this house is practically brand new.

Built it myself just a few years back. Ain't *nothing* wrong with *this* house."

Rayford leaned back in his chair to let the ire cool a bit. He put his forefinger up under his lower lip and tried to look thoughtful.

My grandfather went on. "What I want," he said, "what I'm looking for, is some place up in town. Either that or one down on the river. So's I could go a-fishing whenever I took a notion to. Or if I was in town, I could go to the store or up to the square on my own. In walking distance, you might say." He paused, the muscles in his mouth working his false teeth. "You know of any place like that?"

Rayford was almost dizzy with delight on the one hand and fear on the other. He had never actually bilked anybody in his whole life, at least not on this scale. Here was this old man, not too well in touch with the modern world and practically offering himself up on a platter. Nevertheless, fear convulsed Rayford's guts. He wasn't sure he could pull it off.

"What about your kinfolks?" he asked cautiously. "They live around here?"

"Oh, I got a daughter around here someplace. But that hadn't got nothing to do with anything. I tend to my own business. I don't need nobody telling me what to do or how to do it. I can handle my own business my own self. If you can find me a place to trade, one like I said, then you'll have you a deal, Mr. Renfro. I can guarantee you that."

―――――

MY MOTHER is the kind of person who thinks the world is constantly on the verge of coming unstuck and that it's her personal assignment to keep it glued together—with peanut butter, egg white, confectioners'-sugar frosting, sweat, plasma, spittle and mud, whatever comes to hand. When the world is constantly coming apart, you don't have time to work on a foolproof glue formula. You make do. She's had a lot of experience making do.

She *herds* everyone a lot. She tries to herd them in the same general direction, toward heaven, but, failing that, she at least tries to keep them together here on earth. "This may be the last time we're all together like this," she always says at every holiday gathering or funeral or reunion. Since our flock is large and our ages and circumstances are varied, each time we're together usually is the last time we achieve that particular configuration. I've stopped pointing that out to her, though. She seems to get some comfort just from repeating the phrase, like an incantation—"the last time, the last time." This family is nothing if not rhetorical, and one may as well savor the poignancy of the words even if one can do nothing to alter the situation.

Still, she tries. She lies awake at night making plans. How to reconcile siblings, repair marriages, bring stragglers back to the fold. But for the past five years, ever since my grandfather has been living just across the field from her, he's put a severe strain on her holding-together efforts, many of which have been spent on him. How to hold his soul together with his aging body, his flagging memory with his ossifying brain, himself with his children. Now she suddenly had the additional problem of how to keep him stuck to his house where she could take care of him.

Rayford Renfro had wasted no time finding a little three-room shack down on White Rock Creek, a main tributary of the Trinity River. It was in an area that had been divided into small lots for weekend cabins before the oil bust in Texas put an end to the recreational real-estate market for a while. The place was no more than a half-finished camp house, but Rayford could see that my grandfather didn't put much stock in fancy finishes. I'm not even sure the plumbing worked. At any rate, it had the twin virtues of being worth about a quarter of my grandfather's present place and of belonging to a cousin of Rayford's who lived in Houston and who had been trying to unload it for three years. Rayford offered to take it off his hands for a small finder's fee.

He hoped to trade it straight across to my grandfather for his house. Then he'd simply pay off his cousin's loan in short order with the income from the house.

It wasn't a particularly complicated plan. It was one even Rayford might have been able to pull off if my mother, who monitors every vehicle that pulls into my grandfather's driveway, hadn't gotten suspicious. She managed to wrangle enough information out of my grandfather to guess at what was going on. She's also lived in this county long enough and has sufficiently extensive connections to be able to check up on just about anybody's background. Then too, she works, many times unerringly, through intuition. It didn't take her long to piece together my grandfather's—and Rayford's—scheme. When she discovered it, she was horrified and frightened. She wasn't at all sure that she could handle this particular crisis alone. For one thing, she is loath to act on her own initiative when the problem concerns her father's money. The specter of being seen as the unscrupulous daughter haunts her, even though her siblings, for the most part, prefer to leave everything to her. But this predicament seemed to call for getting them all together, or at least as many of his seven surviving children as possible.

"What's the old geezer up to now? He's not sick, is he?" That's what her brother, the one who's named after their father, asked when she called him.

"Ward," she had said, "you've got to come home," forgetting that forty years ago "home" for him had ceased to be where his father lived. Home to him now was a townhouse not far off the interstate in Winston-Salem. Home was a place even his own children had left.

"No, he's not sick, but I'm afraid he's getting himself into a lot of trouble."

"Don't tell me he's started running around with the ladies, shooting craps—that kind of thing."

My mother is used to this kind of baiting of her Baptist morality; she doesn't let it deter her from her goal. "The kind of trouble I need your help with," she said. "You're in real estate. You'll know how to handle this. And maybe he'll listen to you."

"Me?" He snorted and said something just outside the range of the phone she was glad she couldn't hear.

"He's *got* to stay where he is, Ward. That's the only way Lamar and I can take care of him. As it is, he really shouldn't even be living down in that house alone. He's going to blow himself up with that space heater one of these days. But if he goes off down on the river somewhere, there's not any way I'll be able to look after him. It's not even the money that upsets me so much. I don't care about the money. It's just that that—creature!—is trying to take advantage of him. An old man like that. He can't even see what he's signing."

"Now don't start crying, sis. We're not going to let him do that."

"I've tried to explain it to Dad, how much his property is worth here and how that fellow is trying to cheat him. I even think at one point he was starting to understand what I was talking about. But then he got embarrassed and wouldn't talk about it anymore. He told me it was his money and his property to do with as he pleased."

There was another indistinct epithet on the other end of the line. She waited, squinching up her eyes in prayer.

"Well. Let me call you back this evening. I'll have to check with Pam and see when I can get away. You just pull yourself together now. It's going to be okay."

"All right. Okay. I'm so glad. I really do thank you, Ward. I really do need your help." She put down the phone with a satisfied sigh. The glue had stuck.

———

THAT WAS HOW, on the next Sunday, five of my grandfather's children came to be disposed around my mother's dining table, scraping at the last smears of her chocolate pie on their plates ever more slowly as they realized that the dinner was winding down to the serious discussion part. The old man, who had been persuaded to come over for dinner too, had, as was his custom, stood up as soon as he'd finished his pie.

"I've got to go to the house," he always says.

Then my mother says, "Oh, Daddy, you don't have to go yet."

Then he says, "Yep, I've got to go take my poison," meaning his heart medicine, which in any case he never remembers to take. This is a litany they go through every Sunday.

"See?" my mother says as she shuts the door after him and turns back to the table, raising her arms in the air. "That's the way it is all the time." This is when they start getting nervous.

There is Bess, the widowed nurse; Irene, the alcoholic who, with her third or fourth husband, runs a barbecue place thirty miles away; and Sally, a late-blooming investment counselor who is thinking of taking on a third husband, a man everyone identifies as "the one with the yellow Mercedes."

Then there is Ward, the fifth in order of birth but the oldest son, a small-time entrepreneur in cars, land, and insurance, a trader like his Grandfather Silas, only with a computer instead of a spring wagon. Although he was named for his father, he uses only the middle name. He also looks like a replica of his father at about fifty, except dressed in a suit and tie instead of overalls. He doesn't like attention called to this resemblance— the same angular bones, the thin, straight nose, the mouth that pulls down on one side in a crooked smile.

The other living son is named Parker, after Chief Quanah Parker, the last of the great Comanche chiefs. It's the kind of name you always have to explain to people, though, and after Parker left home and joined the Air Force, he became Hank. He didn't come home for this conference. Ever since his early retirement, he's been trying to raise cattle in the Ozarks. "If he wants to raise cows," my grandfather grumbles, "why don't he come back to Texas to do it? The weather up there's too hard on cattle."

Parker doesn't talk much, not even in person, and hardly at all on the phone. All the messages have to be relayed through his wife. It's hard to make glue stick that way. But my mother always has an excuse ready for her younger brother. "They can't leave those cows, you know. It's calving time." Or else they're branding or selling, depending on the season. And, "Parker's always been so tenderhearted, you know. He just can't bear to see Daddy like this." Being tenderhearted is counted a rare virtue among men in this family, and covers a multitude of sins.

The only other sibling not there was Rachel, who had a stroke last year and still cannot walk. Besides, she gets exasperated with her father, and between them they often have what my mother calls "words." Nevertheless, my mother felt reasonably successful in her roundup. Five out of seven wasn't bad. Most of the time she can only get that many together for a funeral.

"I guess you all know why we're all here today," Ward began. They all fiddled with the silverware nervously; they hadn't expected him to sound so purposeful. As a rule they prefer indirection, even a certain wry irony, whenever they're discussing anything serious.

"I just wanted to bring you all up to date on what's been going on with Dad," he went on. "At least since I've been here this time. Only Esther and Lamar know firsthand all the problems. And I've got to say that after these past few days I don't see how they do it and still retain their sanity." From the way he paused at this point you knew that if this had been an after-dinner speech at the Lions' Club, there would have been a polite spattering of applause. As it was, there was only the fidgety silence of trapped children.

"Esther and I went to her lawyer here to see what we could do about Dad's wanting to trade off his house for some little shack this jerk Renfro found down on the river off of Highway 90."

"That's the road to Trinity, isn't it?" Sally asked. The way she said it, straightening her back and arching her eyebrows, it was as though she were laying down a card in a game. And for every card you played, you got a point. She snapped hers as she laid it on the table so everyone would notice that she had played her turn.

"Now Esther and Lamar, when they sold him this acre, very wisely had a clause put in the contract whereby, if he ever sold it, they'd have first option to buy it back. We had to go to the courthouse and check and see that the note was attached to the deed and that it was all properly recorded."

"I hated going behind Daddy's back like that, but there didn't seem to be any other way to handle it," my mother said, tracing the crease in her napkin with her fingernail.

"Well, there wasn't a thing wrong with that, either," Ward put in quickly. "Courthouse records are a matter of public information. If Joe Blow from Kokomo wanted to waltz in there and find out anything about it, he could, just as easy as you or me." He tried to keep the edge of exasperation out of his voice.

"I understand how Esther would feel, though," Bess said, reaching over to pat her hand.

Irene, who was moving the salt-and-pepper shakers back and forth in little patterns on the tablecloth, said nothing.

Ward took a deep breath and continued. "Since the note had already been paid off, though, we ended up having to go to his safety deposit box at the bank to find it. Esther's on the card to get into the box, you know." He paused. "And if you think it was hard to talk her into the courthouse, you should have seen me persuading her to look in what he calls his lockbox."

There were little ripples of relieved laughter around the table.

"I might also tell you that we found a stack of hundred-dollar bills stuffed in there too. Over $30,000 in all. It seems that Dad's been cashing his government checks and stashing the cash away there."

"You mean the actual cash!" Sally blurted out, sitting bolt upright. "Not even in a CD or anything?"

"That's right. Don't ask me why. I wouldn't even want to speculate. But that's how he does it."

"Why, that's not the worst of it," my mother interjected. "He carries around a roll of hundred-dollar bills in his pocket as big as my fist. Lamar takes him up to pay his light bill, and he takes this roll out and peels off a hundred-dollar bill. Of course, anybody could see him with that and knock him in the head or something. He likes taking it out and flashing it around. He doesn't realize how dangerous it is. This is what just *worries* me so *much*." She clenched her fists over her chest to add emphasis to her words.

They all listened, moving their eyes and the silverware around nervously. They just wished Esther wouldn't get so emotional about it. After all, what are they supposed to do? She's the oldest. She's always taken care of things. So what does she expect them to do?

"Anyway," Ward continued, trying to get them all back on track, "we took the papers to Esther's lawyer, and he assured us this deal wouldn't be able to go through. Then I called up this Mr. Renfro. You should have heard him when I told him this was G. W. Adams, Jr., talking. He started backpedaling just as fast as he could. Said he'd just been trying to help the old guy out and that he hadn't meant any harm. I told him that if he so much as showed his face around here again, we'd have the county attorney on him so fast it'd make his head swim. I told him about the option too, just to make sure it sank in."

"Have you explained all this to Daddy?" Bess asked.

Her brother shrugged. "Any number of times, but just how capable do you think he is of understanding all this? It's not like he's playing with a full deck, you know."

"And he gets embarrassed," my mother put in quickly to smooth over the disrespectful tone. "You can see it in his face. He knows he's not following all the details, and so he gets embarrassed and, well . . ."

"Childish," Sally supplied.

"Now the point is," Ward went on, "I think we've got this immediate crisis under control. We may have some hassle with Dad tomorrow when Mr. Renfro doesn't show up to close the deal like Dad's expecting, but I'm hoping we can make it through all right. Actually, I could have handled the whole thing myself, but it seemed good to have the lawyer's opinion on it, just to let Renfro know we were really on top of things and this wasn't just some doddery old man he was dealing with."

Irene and Bess flinched at the last phrase. "I didn't realize he was in *that* bad a shape," Irene said.

"Now the question is, what are we going to do in the future?" their brother went on, ignoring her. He could feel the focus beginning to dissolve, and a tinge of desperation was creeping into his voice. "I mean, my God, the man's not capable of handling his own finances. Esther here has to check up every month to see that he's paid his light bill so they don't cut his electricity off."

Bess cleared her throat and stacked her spoon on top of her fork on her plate. "The best thing for him, of course, would be a residence home of some sort," she said. "He shouldn't be living by himself in his condition."

Irene got up and started clearing away the dishes from the table and carrying them into the kitchen.

"He and Mother should have gone to that Masonic Home before she died," Sally said.

"He's not about to go there now, I can tell you," my mother said. "And to put him in a nursing home—well, it would kill him. I've already told him I'd never do that. Not as long as I'm able to take care of him."

Irene called from the kitchen. "I'm going on down to Daddy's now. See if he made it all right."

A silence descended on the group around the table till they heard the back door shut and saw Irene making her uneven way down the driveway. One of her legs has a damaged nerve and swings belatedly behind the other.

"I don't like the looks of that," Sally said, crushing her napkin into a tight ball and dropping it rhetorically onto her plate. "She's going down there to tell on us."

Ward frowned. "You may be right," he said. "What the

hell. We can't help that. We're not children anymore. He's the child."

"It's just as well she's gone," Sally said, "because I wouldn't say this while Irene was here. I knew she'd take it the wrong way. You know how she is about Daddy, especially when she's been drinking. And you all may think this is terrible too, but"—she took a deep breath and looked around the table—"I truly believe that it would be merciful if the Lord would just see fit to go ahead and take him. I mean, he's not happy. He must be miserable just sitting down there in that house day after day. He refuses to go to the Grandpersons' Center or any place where he could be with people. And we just can't go down there and camp out. I mean really. He has such unrealistic expectations. Of course, what he wants is for us to come back home and live with him. So I just think it would be the best thing if the Lord was to go ahead and take him." She looked around the table again, made a little nod with her head signaling the end of her speech, and started gathering up the rest of the dishes with an air of finality.

"When he *does* go, it'll probably be because he falls and breaks something," Bess said matter-of-factly. "A hip, maybe. Then he'll have to be hospitalized, and then he'll be sent from the hospital to a nursing home. That's the only way he'll ever consent to go, no matter how bad he gets."

The table fell silent as they all turned over the possible scenarios in their minds. Their father falling down the porch steps, or not waking up some morning, or clutching at his chest as he examined his row of peach trees.

My mother broke the silence. "I certainly appreciate you coming and handling this, Ward. I don't know what I could have done without you." She framed this in a formal way in order to register this event in their memories, like a notary public's seal on an affidavit.

"It's just a drop in the bucket, sis. I know that. It's nothing compared to what you and Lamar do all the time. But I was glad to be able to help."

74

He paused, and his face flushed darker. "Of course, according to him I've never done one thing right in my whole life. Not one thing that I've ever done has he been proud of. Not one word of praise have I ever heard from him. The only way I could have pleased him was to stay on the farm, to keep on following that plow. Well. I got out of there as soon as I could, and I never had any intentions of going back."

"Well," Bess said. She dropped the word into the silence to dilute the tension. "You're his *son*, Ward." She said it as if the word in itself explained everything.

"Don't give me that bull. Was he pleased when I joined the Navy? Hell, no. *He'd* never been in the Navy. But you can be sure that when I signed on that dotted line, it was so I'd never have to go back to his kind of life again. He always *wanted* life to be hard. Just so he could brag about how hard he worked and how tough he was. But to me it was just plain dumb." He paused and gave a little ironic shrug. "I had four kids—three of them boys, for God's sake—and I don't think he even knows their names."

"There's lots of things he doesn't remember anymore," Bess said, as though she were smoothing out wrinkles in a patient's sheet.

"We all left. We had to," my mother added. "He's just lonely these days and doesn't think straight."

And thus the family conference ended. What, after all, had been accomplished? Everything, it was assumed, would go on just as it had before. Rayford Renfro's plans had been short-circuited, but nothing would be any different. My mother and father would have the same problems. She would continue to cry, and he would continue to fume.

"He could come stay with me," Bess had offered. But, of course, he wouldn't. He wants to be in his own house, on his own turf.

The next day the rain had stopped and the sky was clear. My mother had left early that morning to take her brother to the airport, but not before there had been one last row between Ward and his father.

"I just figured out what you came here for," my grand-father had said. "You didn't come to see me at all. You came to help your sister keep me from buying that place I wanted down on the river." And he had stumped out of the room.

After they left for the airport, I walked over to see my grandfather, rehearsing my speech along the red clay road that dips down to the creek. I don't know what I had expected from the family conference myself, but I could see that my parents' plight was not going to be altered by it. I had something still to say to my grandfather. The pine trees that rise up on either side of the road kept their peace.

"I want to talk to you about my mother," I said as soon as I came in.

"What about her?" he said, settling back in the big black chair.

"I'm worried about her."

"Why? Is something wrong with her?" He sounded wary already.

"She's awful upset."

"Well, I reckon I got her riled this morning. I told her I didn't need her nor her brother meddling in my affairs."

"But you do, you know."

"What? What do you mean?"

"I mean you can't handle them by yourself anymore."

"What do you mean, can't handle 'em by myself? I been tending to my own business long before you was born. Or her, either."

"But you're old now. You don't even see well enough to read whatever it is you might be signing."

"That don't make no difference. I don't need nobody's help."

"What if you get sick?"

"If I get sick, I got someplace I can go up in Arlington."

"You mean the Masonic Home?" For some reason, he won't use the name, as though that would bring the reality closer to him. "You'd have to give them everything you've got, you know."

76

"I'd give it away before I went."

"If you did that, you'd have to wait another year before they'd let you in. That's the rules."

"No sir. Not me. They know me there."

I decided to shift my ground. "You know you would have lost your place here if Ward hadn't come and gotten that straightened out."

"I knew what I was a-doing. Ward was just strutting his stuff. He likes to do that."

"But you didn't even know how much this place was worth. Much less the one you were wanting to trade it for. He saved you a considerable amount of money."

"That's all right. It was my money."

"Do you honestly believe your children would stand by and see you cheated like that?" Both of us were making an effort to keep our voices down, but his face was flushed, and he twisted from side to side in his chair. He was trying not to swear, though he had to swallow a word every now and then. He knew his rationality was at issue here, and he was struggling to be convincing.

I kept pressing. "You've got to accept the fact that you do need help now."

"And just how do I need help?"

"Transportation, for one thing. How would you even get your groceries or go to the doctor if it weren't for Mother and Daddy to drive you?"

"I'd get me a jitney to come out here and get me. That's what. I got a telephone. I'd call me a taxi."

I leaned back and shook my head. "Sure. And somebody'd knock you in the head and take that roll of bills off of you that you carry in your pocket."

"I can move to town. Then I won't need no car. I'd be up there where folks knows me."

"Well. All that doesn't make any difference to me, I want you to know. If you want to get knocked in the head or whatever, that's okay by me. But what I do care about is my mother. And

I know all this is driving her crazy. Trying to take care of someone as uncooperative as you."

"Well, that's her problem." He sat back again and snorted. "Un-co-op-er-a-tive!" He said the word syllable by syllable, breaking it down as though he were cracking a dry stick across his knee, something as flimsy and inconsequential as that. Then he snorted again, as though flinging it aside. This was to show me the contempt he had for my thinking that words, mere words, could undo him.

And he's right. Words only work with someone who believes in compromise, in working things out. He's never compromised in his life. He's always said, *Ain't nobody going to tell me what to do,* and walked away. Now he can't walk away anymore, not from age and infirmity, but he still says the same thing.

And he's right, maddeningly right, about my mother. It is her problem.

When I got up to leave, he chuckled, in a good mood now, feeling like he'd won something today. He even felt magnanimous.

"Thanks for coming by to see me." He chuckled again, his broad grin spreading across his bony face.

"Well. Take care of yourself," I said as I opened the door.

He couldn't resist a final jab. "Why? You afraid the boogerman might get me?"

"The boogerman wouldn't have you," I said from the other side of the screen door.

He laughed and slapped his knee. "He might find out he's got holt of a bigger devil than his own self," he said.

ACHIEVERS

MELQUIADES ORTIZ was still farming his land in the Mimbres Valley of New Mexico with a horse-drawn plow at the age of 104.

At seventy-one, Michelangelo designed St. Peter's in Rome and directed its construction till his death at eighty-nine. During this same period, he also painted the frescoes of the Pauline Chapel.

Frank Lloyd Wright completed New York's Guggenheim Museum the year he died, at the age of ninety-one.

Ada Roe ran a dairy store in London till she died in 1970 at the age of 111.

At eighty-one Benjamin Franklin negotiated the compromise that brought about the writing and ratification of the U.S. Constitution.

According to Plutarch, the Roman statesman Cato began his study of Greek at eighty.

Thomas Edison patented his first invention at twenty-one, his last at eighty-one.

When she was eighty-four, Marian Hart flew a single-engine Beechcraft Bonanza alone across the Atlantic.

When he was seventy-four, Marc Chagall began the twelve stained-glass windows for the Synagogue of the Hadassah Hospital at Jerusalem; on his eighty-fifth birthday, he opened the National Museum of the Biblical Message of Marc Chagall in Nice.

Fred Streeter made his last weekly radio broadcast as the BBC's gardening expert at the age of ninety-eight.

In 1972, Charlie Smith of Bartow, Florida, was officially recognized as the oldest living American. He had been forced to retire from his job at a citrus farm in 1955 when, at 113, he was considered too old to climb trees anymore.

Sophocles wrote *Oedipus Rex* when he was sixty-eight. When he was ninety, according to tradition, his son Iophon tried to have him declared senile and incompetent by the Athenian court, whereupon Sophocles produced as his defense the choral ode he had just completed for *Oedipus at Colonus*.

At ninety, Albert Schweitzer was still treating patients in his hospital at Lambaréné in Gabon. However, Paul Weiss, a Yale professor appointed to the Albert Schweitzer Chair at Fordham University, was denied the job because he was over seventy.

The Deserter

IT'S TRUE. They left. And none of them ever intended to return, from the first one—my mother, a tall, thin country girl terrified of the city who nevertheless went to Houston in 1937 to learn typing and shorthand—down to Sally, the last one, who married a high-school ag teacher in 1960 to get away from home. They left, turning their backs not just on their father's home, which in any case never stayed in one place for long, but on a way of life made of taciturn chores, steady rhythms, heat, and weary necessity.

The older girls left to get jobs as secretaries, nurses, bookkeepers. World War II stirred the nation like a spoon, turning all the old ways upside down and redistributing people in unfamiliar places. A decade earlier their father, an experienced worker and a man, had barely found enough work to keep his family together. Now, in a nation at war, it was easy for even young girls just off the farm, like my mother and her sisters, to get jobs.

Not that any of the sisters became riveters or worked on assembly lines. The jobs they took were traditionally ladylike, and with their earnings they bought new clothes, the likes of which they had only dreamed of on the farm—pert white blouses, nylon stockings, spectator pumps. I've seen snapshots of them taken with their Brownie camera—the four sisters and a cousin lying on their backs in the grass with their heads together in the center to make a daisy pattern, an idea they probably got from a movie. They are all smiling up at the camera, fresh and blooming in their new clothes and fashionable hairdos. These are very different from the family pictures taken before the war, which show them with their father and brothers lined up in a row across some grassless, swept-dirt yard, as though they were facing a firing squad, their faces guarded and brooding.

The war caught up with my grandfather just outside Palacios, a little town on the Gulf Coast southwest of Houston where he had rented yet another farm. The town had been a haven for shrimpers and Baptist vacationers who came to spend the summer at a church encampment there. As soon as the war broke out, however, the army set up a training camp just outside the town limits. With several thousand new recruits on its outskirts, Palacios began bursting its seams. Uncle Buck had found work at the army camp as a refrigeration repairman, and as one by one the girls left their father's home, they went to live with their aunt and uncle in town.

"I don't understand," Bess told her Aunt May when she decided she wanted to be a nurse. "Daddy thinks it's not a job for respectable women. I can't believe it. He said he wasn't going to have any daughter of his bathing naked men. He asked me why I wanted to do that kind of thing anyhow, as though it was something dirty and low-down. I just don't understand why he feels like that. My own daddy."

"He's just trying to do the best he knows how by you, honey," Aunt May told Bess. "Just let it be for a year. Come work in the drugstore here in town. Then if he won't give in, we'll see what we can do. Maybe your Uncle Buck and me can come up with the money."

"I hate going against my daddy," Bess said, "but I've got to do something."

This is how change really comes about—not in statistics, not in history books, but in family scenes, around kitchen tables.

82

When my mother sat down in front of her first typewriter, history changed forever, as certainly as when the sirens sounded at Pearl Harbor. And history changed every year my great-aunt's capacious old two-story house on the bay took in another of her brother's children.

It was, in fact, the first home I remember. My mother, a young war-bride whose husband was overseas, moved into the house with her new baby. She worked at the army camp while I spent my days with my great-aunt, who—besides doing the cooking, cleaning, and washing for her houseful of young working girls—also ferried me out to the army camp at noon so that my mother could nurse me during her lunch hour.

Naturally, young soldiers began to call on the sisters, generating an air of constant anticipation and excitement in the house. Someone was always getting dressed up, putting on fresh lipstick, doing her hair, either to go to work or out to the movies. In my grandfather's house no one had ever worn lipstick or gone to the movies.

It was a whole new life for the sisters. They had never been allowed to have callers before. They had lived out in the country, hemmed in by trees and fields, and had had neither the clothes nor the transportation to escape their isolation. Practically their only visitors had been relatives. Then, suddenly, their world expanded. It became a social place, with next-door neighbors, store clerks, Sunday-school teachers, bosses, girlfriends, suitors. They could walk down a sidewalk, open a door, step through it, and people would know their names. They could sing in the choir, go to ice-cream socials, talk on the telephone.

Not that their Aunt May didn't keep a tight rein on them. She lived in mortal dread of something untoward happening to her brother's children while they were in her care. For even though he still had five children at home, he took each departure as a desertion, a betrayal. She knew he was waiting for some disaster to happen that would vindicate his unbending opposition to the modern world. Nevertheless, how could their aunt turn away the four young girls so eager for a wider world, one where there could be friendships, work that seemed easy after the fields, spending money, and the chance of falling in love with a soldier?

And all of them did that too.

My mother, of course, had already met and married hers, the year before the war broke out, at a cousin's house in Houston. The other girls, however, met men at the USO, men from other states, exotic places like South Dakota and New Jersey. Aunt May fretted about these foreigners and how her brother would take to them. But when the time came, he took them stoically, as he had always taken every disappointment. By the end of the war, all his daughters were married and on their way to a kind of life utterly different from what they had known with their father.

And how, after all, do you tell your children what they can do, what they can be, especially when the world is changing so fast?

When my grandfather had come back from World War I, his life had gone on much as it had before he left home. People went back to the land to make a living. Men and women made families with the same expectations that their parents had had. It was a time when people were satisfied just to keep their families together. Making a living was the unremitting theme of life. It underlay every decision, came before every other consideration. Learning, religion, amusement, anything beautiful—these were extras, sometimes even worse than extras. They were a mockery, a humiliation to people enduring hard times. You had to ignore them, or even hate them, to prove you could live without them. Work was the single undisputed virtue. It was the foundation of the world. It made everything else possible.

The most important thing it made possible was keeping your family together. Not being able to keep his family together had been the worst shame that could come upon a man in my grandfather's world. A man who worked all his life and kept his family together had done all that could reasonably be expected of him. If he had time for any extras, that was his business. If he didn't, it was nobody else's. If it made him a harsh man, nobody held that against him.

But with this second war, everything changed. Soldiers, after their discharge, did not go back to the farm but went to the cities to find work. To escape the Depression, many of them, like my father, had joined the army even before the war began. They had no intention of going back to the kind of debt-servitude their fathers had known.

And there were so many things to buy now, things their fathers had never encouraged them to expect from life. Refrigerators, washing machines, automobiles. Insurance policies that promised not just to pay for your burial expenses but to give cash to your survivors. Insurance that protected you if you had to go to the hospital. My grandfather had been about as familiar with insurance as he had with refrigerators. The very concept of making payments to fate, of wiping out risk with money, was foreign to him. His whole life had been nothing but risk. He didn't see how money could have covered any of the losses he had suffered.

But his daughters, along with most of the country, having had their fill of fate, thought money could go a long way toward compensating. It seemed a good idea to them to build as many dikes as possible against that sea of chaos that might at any moment overwhelm the little island of stability they had claimed for their own. If the house burned down (as their father's did three years after the war), they didn't want to have to depend on the kindness of neighbors to put clothes on their children again. For one thing, they continued to change neighborhoods almost as frequently as their father had changed farms. And they couldn't always count on their strange new neighbors to understand that taking up the slack in the social fabric was the way the world had held together. Far better to have an insurance policy to guarantee your safety.

Yet even so, even with insurance, their new world didn't always hold together. Because one thing they found they couldn't insure was marriage.

Rachel was the first to discover this. It was, of course, no more than my grandfather had expected.

She was the one he called "Princess," the one who was his favorite, the youngest of the four sisters living in my great-aunt's house in town. It only made sense to him that she would be the one singled out by fate to be damaged in this way.

Still, after the divorce, she didn't return to her father's house. And at the end of the war, she married again.

Hers was only the first in a long line of uninsured, uncompensated lost marriages among her brothers and sisters. But none of them ever went home to live when a marriage failed, though they would bring their new spouses to visit their father and receive his tacit blessing on their marriages.

Other things changed, too. Important things, like dishes. His daughters had dishes that, instead of having flowers painted on them, were one solid color, colors with names like "avocado" and "burgundy." They bought sofas that made into beds. They took their children to public swimming pools. They joined the PTA. They went to eat at Mexican restaurants. None of them married farmers. And all of them, every one, had more money than he did.

Was it only money that made the difference in these post-war years? If he had had more himself, would he have changed along with the rest of the country? Would he have expected—demanded—more out of life? Would he be sitting alone now in a house that might have been built in 1918, with no television and only one light burning after dark? Would he have adapted, along with everyone else, to affluence, and taken up golf? Why has he found the modern world so unsatisfactory? What is it that he finds in a vanished way of life that he cannot part with, cannot be compensated for?

Whatever it is, in leaving it, his children have left him too. Their loyalty lies with a different age. They tell their children to expect the best, to aim for the top. Be all that you can be. But they've given up hoping that they can hold their families together the way he did.

His three sons left home to join a peacetime army. It was their best bet for an education—not just in technical skills but in acculturation. They wanted to learn how to be part of a country that was becoming more uniform and tolerating less isolation, less singularity. Their father would have been proud to be like his own father, a man he admired and respected—would have been proud to have a life like his. They, however, had no intention of being like their father, who, whatever his personal attributes, did not know how to live among people in cities, did all his business on a cash basis, and intended to go on wearing khaki work-clothes in the sweltering heat the rest of his life.

What did they carry away with them from his house, what wisdom to stand them in good stead? *Pay what you owe. A man's word is his bond.* And most of all, *Don't try to be something you're not.*

But that was exactly what they wanted—to be something they weren't yet. To be a part of what was going on around them. What they had been brought up to be somehow wasn't enough anymore. Who, among their buddies in the Air Force or the Navy, cared if they could hitch up a mule and plow a straight furrow? That didn't matter anymore. Other things mattered now, things they had to learn without their father's help in order to become something they weren't but desperately wanted to be. It didn't have to do with a particular kind of work so much as it did with the context of that work. Except for the son who died young and had wanted to be a doctor, none felt any particular calling to be one thing instead of another. What they wanted was to make a certain amount of money, live in a neighborhood in an acceptable kind of house, and drive a decent car. The work they did to earn this money, however, didn't concern them much, so long as they didn't feel uneasy telling people what it was, so long as they didn't have to explain. The work had to be something people would understand so completely they wouldn't give it a second thought. That wasn't going to be farming.

I REMEMBER when Parker, his middle son, left home. They were living on this hill then, and my grandfather was raising hogs on another forty acres. It was June, and Parker had just graduated from high school. I had come to spend part of the summer with Sally, his last child. Within that secret pact the young make against the old, we knew that Parker had been talking to the Air Force recruiter in town, though he had told neither of his parents. The Korean conflict was over, but the peacetime army was still alluring to young graduates with no other plans than to get away from home as quickly as possible.

What did my grandfather expect? Did he really believe that his son would be content to make the rounds of the cafes in town, collecting the kitchen refuse for the hogs? The kind of farming Parker had learned about in Future Farmers of America at school was a different kind than what my grandfather had practiced all his life.

So when, toward the end of the term, the recruiter—a bluff, hearty man with mild eyes and sandy hair—started coming around, making promises of travel and a vague kind of technical training, Parker had seen this as his way out. His situation wasn't much different—he was a boy looking for excitement—than his father's had been back in 1917, except that there was no war going on. He couldn't know that in ten years' time he'd be dropping bombs from a B-52 over Southeast Asia in a war as different from his father's as the FFA had been from sharecropping.

We sat down to supper that evening at the slick, oilcloth-covered table in the kitchen. Our faces were shining with sweat, and our damp clothes stuck to our skin. My grandfather, who never wore a short-sleeved shirt in his life, had the cuffs rolled up on his work shirt. His face and his neck where the shirt made a V just below the collarbone were tanned a deep reddish-brown. It always startled me to see how vulnerable the white, protected places of his body looked—his hairless forearms, his feet, his chest when he bent over the washbasin to splash water on his face. He was tall and lean then, and the skin stretched firmly over the bones of his forehead and cheekbones. He had branching blue veins on his temples that throbbed when he got angry.

When he had finished spreading the thick flour gravy over the hot biscuits on his plate, he looked up at Parker and Leighton and said, "After supper I want you boys to go over to Brother Hodgson's and get some of that salve for the sow we got down."

"Salve ain't going to do her any good, Daddy," Parker said. He hadn't put much on his plate. "We ought to call the vet to come look at her. I think she might have some kind of parasite."

"Vet?" My grandfather said the word as though a foreign object had somehow found its way into his mouth. "She ain't about to die, is she?"

"No sir. Not now. But salve won't do her any good. We need to find out what's wrong with her for sure before we start treating her. I reckon the vet would know best."

"And I guess you got the money in your pocket to pay that vet to come out here and tell me what's wrong with my own sow?"

"Well, no sir. But I think it'd be worth it in the long run."

"The long run? What does a boy like you know about any long run? It's that kind of long run that'll eat up your profits. We'd end up spending all we might make off of that sow, paying it to a vet to come out here and look at her. That's the long run." He laughed shortly, served himself some beans, and looked around the table as though inviting everyone else to share in the joke.

No one said anything. Parker picked up his glass of iced tea and drank half of it. He set it down, carefully fitting it to the damp ring it had left on the oilcloth. "Dad," he said. "I'm joining the Air Force."

Sally and I looked at one another across the table. This

wasn't the way he'd planned it. He had been intending to tell his father down at the barn when they were alone. He'd already told Leighton and us that afternoon.

"What do you mean, joining the Air Force?" My grandfather had put down his knife and fork now.

"The recruiter, Sergeant Talmadge—I've already signed up with him. I'm going to be leaving for boot camp in ten days."

"Son!" Granny said. Then she picked up a dish towel and held it against her mouth as she began to moan.

My grandfather paid no attention to her. "I see," he said. There was a long pause. Then he said, "I guess you think you're not getting treated right around here. No one pays any attention to your opinion. I guess that's it."

"No sir. That's not it at all. But I've got to go sooner or later. I figure it might as well be now. This recruiter, he's giving me a good deal."

"For the long run, I guess," my grandfather said, emphasizing the words with bitterness.

Parker sat there a moment, his jaw clenched. Leighton stared down at his plate. Sally and I widened our eyes at one another. We hadn't counted on being in on the excitement. This was wonderful. It was like a contest between the two of them. On my grandfather's side was the absolute sovereignty he wielded in his house. No one ever stormed out of the room or spoke disrespectfully to him. There was age; there was experience. But on Parker's side was youth and inevitability. Whatever was said, however bitter, he was going. None of us doubted that.

"Yes sir. Four years, anyway. I get a better deal like that," he finally said.

"Deal?" my grandfather said. "When I joined the army, we didn't make no deals. They was a war to fight, and they wadn't no deal about it. We didn't make *deals*."

Granny was still moaning and rocking back and forth in her chair. She'd pushed her plate to the middle of the table.

"Well sir." There was a pause. "I guess it's different now. Like everything else."

Nobody ate much more after that, and nothing else was said. When my grandfather finished what was left on his plate, he tipped his chair back, rocking the back legs from side to side as he always did, and left the table.

Parker said, "I'll go get that salve for you, Daddy," but my grandfather didn't reply. He walked on out as though he hadn't heard him.

Sally and I had to wash the dishes while Granny cleared the table. She slammed the drawers shut and sloshed boiling water from the kettle into the dishpan so that we had to snatch our hands back to keep from being scalded.

As soon as we were finished with the dishes, we slipped out the back kitchen door and around to the front porch, where Leighton sat braiding some leather strips together into a lanyard.

"Where's Parker?" we asked. He shrugged.

"Where's Daddy?"

"Gone to get that salve."

"He didn't send you?"

"He wouldn't let me go."

"When you graduate, are you going to join the army too?" I asked. That was only two years away.

"No," Sally said. "Leighton's going to be a doctor, and we're going to live together and I'll keep house for him. He's not going off like Parker. Isn't that right, Leighton?"

"Sure," he said.

PATRIARCHS

MOST OLDER PEOPLE in the world live close to their children. In China, despite the disruption of traditional Confucian ethics by political upheavals in the mid-twentieth century, almost all old people still live with their sons and their families. Recently one researcher studying a commune of 40,000 found only ten older people living apart from their own families. Even in industrialized Japan, the same Confucian ethic still results in three-fourths of all older parents living with their adult children.

Some contemporary African tribes sustain patriarchal patterns of family residence and property ownership similar to those of the ancient Hebrews, Greeks, and Romans. Among the Sidamo of Ethiopia, the Chaggas of northern Tanzania, the Zulus of South Africa, and the Swazi, power resides in the oldest head-of-the-family. Although younger members of the tribes accede to this arrangement, knowing they will eventually inherit that position themselves, they sometimes reveal ambivalent feelings toward their elders. Generational conflicts commonly arise over inheritance and use of farmland. Such conflicts between father and son have been known to lead to patricide in Uganda and accusations of witchcraft among the Korongo of the Sudan.

According to a 1975 study in the United States, four out of every five older persons had adult children. Only 18 percent of these parents lived in the same household with their children, however. In both British and American communities, about twice as many older parents had daily contact with daughters as with sons. Between 1964 and 1984 the numbers of old people living alone had increased by 123 percent.

A woman delegate to a U.S.–Chinese writers' conference in 1982 hesitantly asked the American author Annie Dillard this question: "The old people in the United States—they like to live alone?"

The Land

DESPITE THE FACT that he has worked any number of jobs, and even though carpentry is what he claims to like best, my grandfather has spent more years farming than in any other occupation. It is working the land that has shaped his life.

But the land he worked was never his own during those years when he was raising nine children on a succession of dirt farms from Teague to Splendora to Palacios, names embedded in my mind like Sinai and Hebron and Jericho were in the minds of the wandering Israelites.

His was the first generation of sharecroppers in the family. His own father, Silas Adams, had come to Texas, carried on the tide of emigrants from the southeast that in one year—1872— deposited a hundred thousand new settlers in the state. Silas was only eighteen then, and, as the youngest of ten siblings, he would not have stood to inherit much of his family's land back in Georgia, anyway. So when he read the advertisements circulating along the eastern seaboard—broadsides claiming that no money was needed to secure a good farm in almost any part of Texas, only "good character, industrious habits, and one or two boys"— he set out to seek his fortune in this land of promise. He found the land, if not the fortune, in Houston County, homesteading two hundred acres on the east side of the Trinity River.

94

Most homesteaders arrived poor and had to borrow money to buy seed, equipment, and supplies to put in a crop. Since Texas law forbade the seizure of homestead land for payment of debts, all the farmer had to offer the bank for security was his crop in the field. Thus the interest rates were unimaginably high, sometimes as much as 60 percent. For many of the emigrants, the dream of starting over turned into a nightmare of debt and loss in that first generation. It's hard to discover any more details about Silas's experience as a homesteader. Refugees don't carry many records with them, and they keep their memories to themselves.

I asked my grandfather about his father one Sunday afternoon. My grandfather's denture plate had cracked, and this was causing him to salivate so much that he had to stop after every few words and wipe his mouth with his handkerchief.

"One day I went to town with my daddy," he recalls. "We put the team and wagon up in the wagon yard, the way you did then, and then my daddy, he stood around on the square talking with the other men. Naturally, I was just a little bobtail boy, but I liked to hear what the grownups had to say. They was all a-going round the circle, the men standing there, you understand, telling why each one had happened to come to Texas. At last ever'one had told his story excepting my daddy. So somebody spoke up and asked him for his story.

"'Well, sir,' he said"—and my grandfather pauses, the same way Silas would have, to add weight to what's coming next—"'when I come to Texas, that wadn't a question you ever asked a man.' Now that was the end of his reply. He didn't say no more about it. And I never asked him, neither."

The lesson is implicit. One stands guard over one's memories in the same way one honors the dead. To keep information private is a sign of respect, a tribute to the fact that the essence of one's experience is beyond sharing, is forever one's own painful treasure. To intrude on that privacy is to demean its worth.

He settles his teeth in his mouth again and leans forward

in the chair so that he can get to the big white handkerchief in his hip pocket. He wipes his mouth, studying all the while on how he's going to add to this story. I can tell he's not finished yet because he keeps his eyes focused on a spot in the floor the way he does when he wants to indicate that there's more to come.

"I did hear tell about some Adams that come to Texas. I can't recall just which one it was, though. Must have been some time earlier. Some Union soldiers had been quartered in the field across from their house back in South Carolina. Or maybe it was Georgia. One or the other. Anyhow, the officers come over to the house, and they was invited in and treated tolerably hospitable. One of the young officers, he picked up a watch that was a-laying there on the mantlepiece. The man of the house told this young gentleman that that there watch belonged to his wife, and he'd be obliged if he'd let it be. But the officer said, 'Mister, your wife ain't nothing now.' And the man, the owner of the house, he pulled out his six-shooter and shot the officer dead. Right there. Well, they put him in the guardhouse, but he escaped in the night. Come to Texas."

So this is what we do with private stories. We turn them into legends. Conflate experiences, attribute them to some shadowy ancestor, some single Adams who stands for many. We don't share; we shape—shape memory into stories.

It seems that Silas, while raising a family of ten children, managed to avoid the debt bondage that befell many farmers during his lifetime. He hung onto his two hundred acres of homestead land—not grand by Texas standards—for sixteen years, until my grandfather was born. Then he sold the homestead and moved his family to Palestine, a county seat, where he bought a store and a small truck farm. His oldest boy remembered sitting on top of the wagon, chairs and quilts piled around him, as the family pulled away from the homestead. When the house disappeared around a bend in the road, he vowed that he would come back someday and buy the farm again.

But being a small-time merchant proved hardly more secure for Silas than being a cotton farmer. He left the store in charge of his wife, the farm in charge of the older boys, and began to travel the country roads in his spring wagon, peddling his goods to isolated farm wives, most often not for cash but for whatever they had to offer in barter.

"He was a trader," my grandfather says. He prefers the racier term "trader" to "peddler."

But though Silas stayed in Palestine for a number of years, he eventually moved on, and always to ever-smaller holdings, especially after the boys necessary to operating a farm grew up and left home.

"It seems like people did an awful lot of moving around from one place to another then." I offer this comment to my grandfather, hoping he may expand on the subject.

"Most folks will try to better themselves," he says, obviously wanting to make this generalization his explanation.

"But it doesn't seem like things *got* any better."

"Well, sister. I tell you. They's all sorts of circumstances that can make a fellow dissatisfied." He does not elaborate. The details of those circumstances are not for public viewing.

It's not hard to come up with any number of reasons for dissatisfaction in such circumstances, depending on one's background and temperament. In the fifty years between the end of the Civil War and our entry into World War I, civilization had not borne much fruit in Texas. Life was still pretty much a matter of simply surviving from one year to the next, from one crop to the next.

Education usually skipped at least one generation, most often the first one born in Texas. There was no mandatory public education in the state then. What schools it had were locally supported and governed. Parents who had to keep their children out of school to work in the fields or tend the babies could hardly admit to themselves—or to their children—what those children were missing. They had to cultivate an air of indifference, if not outright hostility, toward learning. In a good many families, everyone had to work or everyone would starve. And even with all hands working, it was often hard to keep ahead of starvation. This is what being shaped by the land means too.

Silas, who had been educated back in Georgia, was a deacon in the Baptist church and sometimes the church clerk. He often served as a trustee for the local school. However, my grandfather, the youngest boy and one of the last left at home, often had to lay out of school to work in the fields. After all, it was not a society that offered much scope for exercising an education, even supposing one managed to acquire one.

Still, Silas Adams' education back in Georgia had meant that he didn't need to rely solely on cropping when he came to Texas. It was far easier and pleasanter to load his wagon with stalks of bananas and bolts of yard goods he picked up at the train depot and travel the back roads as a trader than to follow a team of mules up and down endless furrows of cotton.

Silas died in 1932, having always lived in a house built on land that he owned. His oldest son had, by then, bought back the original homestead in Houston County, just as he had vowed he would. He used the $1300 he got from the railroad for an axle-oiling device he had invented.

But my grandfather, the youngest son, had no such luck. When he came back from World War I and married my grandmother, there was no land for him. He was then just about the same age his father Silas had been when he first came to Texas, only now there were no more homesteads to be had. So he went to work making a living for his young family doing "first one thing and then another," as he puts it—coal-mining near Lovelady, tying out cotton at the gin, guarding convicts, painting railroad cars, and loading lumber at the sawmill. But Texas was still a rural state then, and farming was always the backdrop, the medium of life. Whenever times were hard or you got laid off at the mill, farming was what you turned to. That was the work that was still possible.

Most of the world's crops have always been produced by some kind of peasant class, whether they are called peons, peasants, serfs, slaves, crofters, or collective farmers—people who do not own the land they work. The cotton South itself had been successful only because of the plantation system. The only change in that system after emancipation was the replacement of black slaves with both black and white sharecroppers.

I used to think that tenant farmers and sharecroppers were the same thing, but they're not. Tenant farmers were a cut above sharecroppers. Tenants owned their own work animals, usually mules, and their plows and other equipment. Sharecroppers had to rent even their tools from the landlord. Tenants could either pay a "standing rent" in currency or farm on the "third and fourth" system, meaning the landlord got a third of the corn and a fourth of the cotton the tenants grew. Sharecroppers (who had no equipment or animals) farmed "on the halves." They got half of what they grew, and the landowner got the other half as rent on the land and equipment.

"Sharecropper" isn't a word that people like to apply to themselves or even to their ancestors. I've never heard my grandfather call himself a sharecropper, although he often talks about farming "on the halves." And when I went to the local library to find some books on the subject, the librarian, who also grew up in this county, assured me that by 1930 all the white people in Texas owned their own land; only black people were still sharecroppers then, she said.

But the book I checked out documented a different story. In 1938, two-thirds of all the tenant farmers in the South were white, and half of all white farmers were tenants.

The land tends to get romanticized today since most people are so far removed from it. How many have dragged a cotton sack, longer than their own length, up and down between the rows in the blazing sun, snatching the fat, fraying fleece from the crackling brown bolls, the five-pointed sepals splayed out like rusty stars, and at each point a thorn? Some workers picked crawling on their knees to keep from bending nearly double over the row. The champion pickers, big men with long arms, straddled a center row and picked a row on each side as well, their arms moving like pistons, keeping up a driving rhythm, stuffing the long sacks that trailed along over the hard, broken clods behind them. It took several children, of course, to equal one adult picker. Wives picked too, leaving the baby on a pallet in the shade, watched over by another child too young to pick. The families started as early in the morning as the chores could be finished, broke at noon to eat cold cornbread and buttermilk in the shade, and staggered on under the pitiless afternoon sun.

Still, a cotton row is something to measure yourself against. The high-sided wagon and the scale wait at the edge of the field. You're working against time, heat, and weariness, but the reward is immediate, visual, measurable. Weighing in with the heaviest sack is satisfying. And at the end of the day you have a sense of conquest; nothing looks as sorry as a stripped cotton field. The stalks may have hung heavy and white as the dew lifted off the field in the morning, but by evening there are only rattling, stripped skeletons still standing. A man could feel he had done something when he and his family had planted and chopped and picked a field of cotton, even if that field was not his own. My grandfather talks about "making a crop" the way I talk about writing a book, with the same sense of satisfaction and completion.

He refuses to say much about the men who did own the fields. "Landlord" is a word he avoids as much as he does "sharecropper." The only comment I've managed to pry out of him about his landlords is that some were better than others. It was not his habit to complain against the owner, at least as long as the owner left him alone to work the land the way he saw fit.

Nevertheless, one can hear chilling tales about landlords turning out families who were farming on the third-and-fourth system and replacing them overnight with other, more desperate families willing to pick the crop on the halves, or for even less. The sheriff would show up and evict for trespassing the tenants who had grown the crop. There was rarely any written contract to protect them.

Some landlords would extend more credit to their renters than others. My grandfather always liked those who provided an open tab for him at the general store. He liked the feeling of walking in and ordering up whatever he wanted. It made him feel—at least for the moment—expansive and provident. This kind of credit was the undoing of many families, though, and probably didn't do his any good.

Still, as I say, my grandfather even now does not talk against his old landlords. To do so would be to acknowledge a subservient position, as though one were a child complaining about a parent.

On the other hand, he does describe for me the best land-lord he ever had, who, he says, "couldn't a treated me better if I'd a been his own boy. I guess he must a been a millionaire, but I never would a knowed it while I was with him."

"I was farming on the shares for him down in the river-bottom. I mean it wadn't no further from my front door to the riverbank than it is from here to the other side of my driveway out there." He points to the road that runs in front of his house now. "Only time I ever lost a crop. The water come up and just floated away my *en*-tire crop down the river, pretty as you please. There I was, sitting on that rich riverbottom land, and all I made off of it was a half a bale of cotton—and I mean off the whole blooming thing. The rest just floated down the river. That, or just rotted on the stalk.

"There I was, in debt to that man. I owed him for my seed and supplies and all, you see. Well. He come out to the place and he says to me, 'Adams, you got too fine a family to keep down here on the riverbottom.' You see," he looks at me sharply, "even your mother was still at home then. 'You need to take these children out of this riverbottom,' he says to me. 'You need to get you a job for wages.'"

"So I told my wife, I said, 'Pack ever thing up. We're moving in to Fostoria.' That was where they was a sawmill, you see—biggest mill around. So I went in there to the office and told 'em I wanted to see Mr. Dunham. You see, he owned the farm I'd been working, and he owned the sawmill too. Well, the man out there, his assistant, he said, 'Mr. Dunham can't see you.

He's a busy man.' But Dunham, he heard my voice from his office and he called out, 'Let that man come on in here. I want to see him.'" My grandfather pauses to drag his handkerchief from his hip pocket and wipe his mouth again.

"So I went on into his office and told him I was looking for work, like he'd advised me. He said, 'Man, don't you know there's people out there a-walking the streets of this town looking for work that's growed up here, lived here all their lives?' But he put me to work anyway, helping the millwright. 'Course, the millwright didn't have too much to do those days his own self." He laughs shortly and leans forward to replace the hand-kerchief.

"'Fore long, my soldier's bonus check come, and I paid Dunham what I owed him for the seed and the supplies. He met me coming off my shift one morning and shook my hand and told me to go across the street to the cafe and have breakfast on him. 'Then you go on over to Cleveland to the Ford place—or Chevrolet, whichever one you want—and buy you a brand-new truck and trailer. I want you to go to hauling lumber for me all over the state.'

"I looked at him and I said, 'Man, I just finished paying you what I owe you, and I ain't a-looking to get into debt again soon.'

"'You just go on and write them a check for it,' he said. 'I already told the bank to cash that check.' But I told him, 'If I knew I'd live long enough to pay you off, I wouldn't even wait to eat breakfast. I'd go on and get that truck now. But don't neither one of us know that.' I went on and ate breakfast, but I never did go get that truck. And sure enough, he was dead inside of a year. Turned out he had a heart condition."

He tells the story with just the barest hint of regret in his voice, as though recognizing he had passed up his one chance to break free of being a poor man. But getting out of debt had, by then, become such an end in itself that he couldn't see any other way of doing.

So Mr. Dunham died, my grandfather moved on, and his

oldest child graduated from high school and left home. She had gone to sixteen different schools in eleven years. The grass had always been greener—or the cotton heavier—in the next county, on another bottomland farm. She went to work in the Sears mail-order department in Houston, a tall, angular girl, frightened of the city but leaving behind forever those long cotton rows baking in the summer heat.

It wasn't until late in the New Deal period that government loans were made available to farm tenants so that they could buy the land they worked. Before that, money had been loaned only to farmers who already owned land. To get a loan, the tenant had to agree to a "farm and home development plan" worked out by a county supervisor that laid out not only what land should be planted in which crop, but also how the farm wife should run her kitchen and her henhouse.

Eight years after the loan program was started, the Bureau of Agricultural Economics was commissioned to make a survey of the attitudes of the borrowers. Most of them said they paid little or no attention to the farm-and-home management plan. On the other hand, they said that they liked to have the supervisor come and visit. In fact, many complained about not seeing more of him.

"Do you think you would have run your farm any differently if you had not had these farm and home plans?" the government supervisor asks in the transcript of one such investigation.

"No, I don't think so," the farmer answers.

"Why is that?"

"Well, I always farmed the land the best I could under the circumstances anyway."

"Is there anything about the plan that seems like a nuisance to you and of no use?" the investigator probes.

"Well, this here planning ahead for the future—as far as that's concerned, I figure that's more or less of a nuisance. I can't figure where there'd be any great benefit out of it. I don't like to figure at what I'm going to get and then not get it."

"Is the supervisor a help to you, or could you get along just as well without him?"

"I believe we could get along just as well without him. But you have to have a head somewheres, I reckon."

"What does the supervisor do when he comes to see you?"

"Smokes ten cigarettes and visits."

"How do you feel about having him come to see you?"

"I like to have him come out. I like to have anyone come out and visit, as far as that's concerned."

But it was not the reforms of the Roosevelt era or the novels of John Steinbeck or Margaret Bourke-White's photographs turning sharecroppers into an aesthetic experience for the leisure class that changed the lives of tenant farmers forever. It was tractors. Between 1930 and 1938, the number of tractors in Texas tripled, and each tractor took the place of from three to five tenant families. By the time my mother graduated from school and left home for Houston, tenant farming was already passing from the scene.

It was at the end of World War II, for the first time in his life, that my grandfather bought his own land. The farmhouse caught fire the second year and burned to the ground. So he traded the land—forty acres—for a house and lot in Houston. Like his father before him, he tried making a living there as a peddler, selling country cures—liniments and salves—to other farm people displaced in the city.

There, for the first time in their lives, his two remaining sons had actual spending money of their own from paper routes. His daughter could walk to a grade school in the neighborhood. His wife made friends with the next-door neighbors, and the emotional instability that had plagued her on those isolated dirt farms faded.

But the migration was not good for my grandfather. He suffocated in the city. He needed the great yawning distances between houses, the emptiness filled only with dark treetops or fields of heavy wet furrows. Some species of birds are like this.

They must be the only one of their kind within a certain radius. My grandfather too needed space around him. He needed to feel it pushing against him, a positive force like a molding thumb on clay. And he needed to push against it too, to hoist the burden of his loneliness and singularity. So, after a year in the city, my grandfather moved his family back to the dearth and isolation of the land.

The land belongs to itself and does not need the people. It would go on growing loblolly pine and Spanish sword and honeysuckle and melting them all back into itself again without the help or notice of man. That's what all that space my grandfather needs is made of: the regardlessness of the land. From the beginning, the people who came here were determined to own this land. Even the Comanches wanted it as their exclusive hunting grounds and fought to keep other tribes out.

Nevertheless, people have not wanted to exploit it so much as to break in upon its austere, inner concentration. That's why its outposts, those weathered board farmhouses with yellow lights showing at the windows after dark, were called "places." In the city, houses have addresses. In the country, people locate themselves by reference to "the Watson place" or "the Czech's place" or "Brother Bruce's old place," even when no one lives there anymore and there is maybe only an old well or a few crepe myrtle trees left to mark it as once a human habitation. "Places" are not artificial points on a grid, like addresses in a city; they are exertions of energy, a striving with some otherwise regardless power, a Peniel.

It is on some hillside, with space all around him, that a man asks, "What is man that thou art mindful of him?" My grandfather's answer has not been the same as the psalmist's, but he has nevertheless asked the question. Or rather, the space, the emptiness, has put the question to him.

You walk along a track of wet leaves in wintertime, the rifle barrel close to your ear; you stop to listen for a squirrel in the branches overhead, your warm breath making a wreath around your face in the cold air. And there, with the blood

105

beating in your ears, your very exhalation visible, the question is inescapable. It distills out of the air with your own breath. There is nothing to distract you from it, no other faces or lives with their own obvious and varied answers. When you live in such a space, isolate, "What is man?" means "What am I?" The question is unavoidable and terrifying.

So that, when I say that my grandfather was shaped by the land, I don't mean that he has an attachment to a particular place, a devotion to an ancestral home. He has been as nomadic as the Israelites, roaming in the desert for forty years. He was shaped by the land in the way that people who survive by outwitting the weather have to be—cautious, observant, set for resignation, for not expecting too much. As the man answering the government survey said, he doesn't like to figure at what he's going to get and then not get it. When you live off the land, you have to be continually getting yourself ready for disaster so that you're not overwhelmed by it when it comes. That's my grandfather's answer to "What is man?"

Life as a season of sowing and reaping has always been an obvious analogy to human experience, one that comes naturally to people who have started every spring by putting seed in the ground and then sweated out weather and blight until the crops were in. That's the way my grandfather has understood life. It won't ever be an easy analogy for us anymore. At best, it will be superficial, antique, not a matter of life and death.

This spring he put some seeds in the ground and I wouldn't be surprised if it was for the last time. It's almost July now, and for a month he hasn't even gone out to hoe the single pitiful row of corn and the one short row of tomatoes. For the first time he doesn't have the strength for it. Instead, he sits in his chair and stares out at the road, hoping for someone to come, some secret fruit from the life he's sown to appear, for the work he's put in to manifest its harvest. And getting himself ready for a disappointment.

ECONOMIES

AGRICULTURAL SOCIETIES generally provide for their older members comparatively well; not only does the food supply tend to be ample and fairly predictable, but the people are geographically stable. In such cultures, families ordinarily care for their own aged members, perhaps because the land most often remains under the control of parents until their death. In fact, so powerful is the older generation among the Sidamo in Ethiopia—who keep sheep and goats and cultivate bananas and maize—that anthropologists have labeled their society "gerontocratic." In rural Ireland, sons work as unpaid laborers on their fathers' farms, dependent and unable to marry, sometimes until their forties. The People's Republic of China, still an agricultural society in 1950, declared in the Marriage Law enacted that year that "parents have the duty to rear and educate their children; the children have the duty to support and to assist their parents. Neither the parents nor the children shall maltreat or desert one another."

In societies with economies that depend on collective work such as fishing, hunting, and foraging, aged members are cared for by communal sharing. This is especially true in regions of the world with severe climates. Inuits, Lapps, Siberian tribes, Navahos, and the Xhosa of southern Africa sustain their older members in this fashion. The Bushmen of the Kalahari Desert in southern Africa live by hunting giraffes and eland and digging tubers. They have little opportunity, and seemingly little desire, to accumulate property. They must move frequently and take with them only such weapons and digging sticks and ornaments as they can carry. When they die, these are scattered on their burial site. Nevertheless, despite their lack of economic leverage, their old people are never abandoned by the community.

England's Poor Law of 1601 was the first organized effort by a state to care for elderly citizens. For the first time, assistance of the aged was determined by geographic area—in this case by parishes—rather than by either family or community relationships. The first social-security system providing a cash payment to compensate for loss of income began in Germany in 1880. Great Britain's Royal Commission on the Poor Laws established old-age pensions in 1908. The U.S. Social Security Act of 1935 set up the Federal Old Age Insurance system. By 1977, 114 nations provided some form of state-managed old age and survivors' insurance; most of these programs are based on a means test.

By 1972, 44 percent of workers in corporate industry in the United States were contributing to private pension plans. In 1980, only 21 percent of the retired population received income from this source.

In 1900, when the United States still had a largely agricultural economy, two out of three older men were still actively employed. In 1984, only one out of every six was still working past sixty-five. Also in 1984, 73 percent of old people living alone had incomes under $7,000. Social Security checks are now the major source of income for most old people in the United States.

The War

ABOUT NOON on Veterans Day my mother's Pontiac pulls up in my driveway and the horn honks.

Veterans Day used to be called Armistice Day when it was still always celebrated on November 11.

The second week in November the grass is still green in Texas, although a strong north wind is stripping the star-shaped leaves from the sweetgum trees today. I put on a flannel shirt as I step out onto the porch to see what my mother wants.

"Can you go over and help your daddy?" she calls out the car window. "My art class starts in fifteen minutes." She takes a bite out of a peanut-butter sandwich as if it were raw meat.

"Your face is all red. What's the matter?"

"Your grandfather took it into his head this morning to burn all those brush piles around his house. Those trees and saplings that David cleared out for him last spring."

"He's burning brush in this wind? It must be blowing thirty miles an hour anyway."

She snatches another bite out of her sandwich and closes her eyes in resignation as she chews. "The two of us, your father and I, have been down there all morning, trying to keep the fires under control. I just begged Daddy not to do it today. I said, 'Dad, if you'll just wait for a day that's not so windy, the very next one, then Lamar and I'll be down here to help you, I promise.'"

"But there must be a dozen or more of those brush piles. And they're higher than my head."

"And nothing would do him except to set them on fire all at one time."

"That's crazy. This is no day to be burning brush. It could catch the whole woods on fire. Your house even. Or his. The neighbor's." I throw up my arms.

"Tell me about it. I tried reasoning with him, but you know just about how much good that did." She swallows the last of her sandwich and wipes her mouth with a yellow Kleenex. "Anyway. I've got to go. And your daddy needs to get on back to the house and take his heart medicine. He's supposed to sell poppies this afternoon at Wal-Mart for the Disabled Veterans. If you could just go over there and watch to see that those brush piles don't flare up again in this wind. They're all more or less smoldering now, but you never know. If a gust was to catch one just right . . ." She shakes her head. One of her favorite phrases is "you never know," delivered with a rising inflection at the end. She adds that now to finish off the sentence.

My grandfather's house sits on an acre of ground at the northwest corner of my parent's land. He built the house—or rather had it built this time—several years ago, after his wife died and he wrecked his pickup, which left him without companion-ship or transportation in a little farmhouse twenty miles from town. For some time before the accident, ever since his sight had started to go, he had been driving with his right wheels off the pavement so that he could feel his way along. When he got out of the hospital after the wreck, my mother brought him home to live with her and my father.

He would get up at five o'clock every morning and sit in the dark living room, waiting for dawn and whispering over to himself his mental calculations of how many board feet he'd need to build a new house. It would be a rectangle this time, bisected both ways into four equal rooms.

After he moved into the house, the timber that had been growing up on that acre for the past forty years began to bother him. He finally got my husband to clear it for him.

"I've got to have room to grow me a crop," he insisted.

"You want *every* tree down?"

"Ever last one."

They had lain there—every oak, gum, hickory, and pine sapling—drying all summer, gradually settling into brown hangouts for snakes and rabbits.

Now on this November morning he had showed up at my parents' house before breakfast. "I just thought I'd let you know I'm going to be burning those brush piles today."

My mother put her cup down. "Now Daddy, don't do that. Wait till the wind dies down."

"No," he said, putting his hat back on, "today's the day. Got to get it done today." And he took off across the field again.

They had hurried out after him, with no breakfast, pulling on their jackets and old boots.

The flames are burning low when I get there, the trunks and limbs like ashy, glowing skeletons. My father has raked all the pine needles away from the fence line on the north side, making about a five-foot firebreak between my grandfather's field and the neighbor's tall stand of timber. His face is flushed.

"I got this throw rug here soaked in water," he tells me. "Just leave it here on this fence post handy. Then if you see the fire get loose anywhere, you can beat it out with the rug."

He hands me a rake. "He set fire to them all at one time," he says grimly. "All at one time. All except the one on the south side there, closest to our house. He couldn't get that one to catch. I guess the Lord still answers prayers after all." His face is gray, and he picks up his jacket and starts toward his own house, disappearing into the smoke across the burning field.

I stand on a sweetgum stump, leaning on the rake and watching the brush piles. Every now and then a branch will give way and fall into the coals. Then the fire will blaze up again for a moment when the wind catches it. The scene looks the way I imagine fires would after a bombing or a battle, the smoke thick and drifting across a battlefield.

━━━━━━

Armistice Day commemorated the end of World War I, also known as the Great War until a later one came along to dwarf it. Armistice—a quaint-sounding word nowadays—came in 1918 on the eleventh hour of the eleventh day of the eleventh month, when the guns finally fell silent along the Western Front. For four years the infantries of Belgium, France, England, Canada, Australia, New Zealand, India, and South Africa had been pounded to pieces in the trenches by the superior German artillery. From Laon, a French city cut off behind the Hindenburg Line, an awesome German gun lobbed shells into Paris, fifty miles away. At the Somme, over a million men bought six miles of earth with their lives.

For three full years the United States had managed to stay out of the war. In 1917, when German submarine attacks on our ships finally forced us into it, my grandfather was twenty years old, restless, and eager to see the world.

The American military was largely a do-it-yourself operation in 1918. Individuals with past soldiering experience took it upon themselves to raise companies of volunteers when war was declared. These volunteers were mostly farmboy adventurers, anxious to see more of the world than the furrow they had been following all their lives.

"Captain Kit McConnico," my grandfather always says, savoring the alliteration and the rhythm of the name. "That was my old commander. He'd already seen service in the Philippines. And he raised my company, Company M of the Fifth Texas Regiment. Two hundred and sixty-seven men. The largest company of volunteers ever raised."

"Were they all from Lufkin?" I always ask. His family had lived there then.

"Lufkin and the little communities around there. Wells, Keltys, Clausen. All from Angelina County, anyhow. Times was hard, and a lot of those boys knew they'd be getting a heap better vittles in the army than what they could get at home."

Company M, still officially a part of the Texas Guard, trained locally for a few weeks until they could be moved to a training center for the national army. They drilled with broom handles and swaggered around town; the local ladies' church societies gave them picnics and parties.

"One day my two brothers, Hoyt and Alver, showed up," he continues. "They was going to volunteer too. You see, they figured the government was going to start drafting men soon, so it was better if we at least all stayed in the same outfit together. But Captain McConnico, he wouldn't take them. Both of 'em were married, you see, and had young families coming up. 'You boys just go on home,' he told them. 'One Adams is enough for this army.' He promised to see to it that they weren't drafted later. And they never were."

Company M was first sent to Camp Bowie near Fort Worth to train. They were there for several months, learning the new weaponry, primarily the ingenious Browning automatic rifle, which was put together entirely with pins so that it could be field-stripped in seconds and the parts scattered if the soldier was in danger of being captured. In fact, the Allies were so worried about this new rifle falling into the hands of the Germans that most of the U.S. troops were issued only the French Chauchat.

By my grandfather's own account, the company of volunteers from Angelina County was a rough bunch. Fights broke out in the ranks as they tried to learn drill maneuvers. One of the company's sergeants had his fingers cut off by an irate private. "Grabbed the bayonet right out of the scabbard where it hung on the bunk."

The young Texans weren't used to being ordered about, at least not by strangers. "And before they shipped us overseas, they always assigned us a new set of officers. You see they was afraid somebody might be harboring a grudge left over from training camp. Some of them men vowed they would get their revenge. So they switched out the commanders before they sent us into combat."

Company M now became a part of Company D, 36th Division, 143rd Regiment of the American Expeditionary Force. They arrived in France only a few months before the war was over. By then, General Pershing had already had it out with Marshal Foch, the commander of the French army, who had at first insisted on controlling the combined Allied forces himself. Pershing, however, unimpressed with what Foch had been able to accomplish thus far in the war, refused to put his men at the French marshal's disposal. Although Foch had stopped the Germans at the Marne in the first year of the war, for the next three years his disastrous frontal assaults against the invincible German guns had resulted in the slaughter of hundreds of thousands of men while achieving no appreciable advantage. As Winston Churchill described the war at that point, the two sides were like a couple of exhausted fighters, leaning against one another for support.

Pershing wasn't about to commit his forces to such a strategic nightmare. In the compromise he and Foch worked out, Pershing retained control of the American Expeditionary Force, but was also assigned the most difficult part of the front—the Argonne Forest. Up to that point, none of the Allied troops had even attempted a drive through the tangled undergrowth of these dense woods. Thus the Germans had had three years to settle in and dig a network of trenches that extended twelve miles back from the front line.

Pershing began his attack through the Argonne Forest on September 17, 1918. My grandfather was accustomed to hunting in the thick underbrush of the East Texas piney woods. He was better off than most of the troops, who, as draftees, some only two months in the army, hadn't yet been trained to load their rifles. Despite the raw condition of his men, Pershing issued orders to advance through the dense woods "without regard of losses and without regard to the exposed conditions of the flanks." Entire units disappeared into the forest, where they were cut off from one another. The Germans, secure in their underground warrens, then counterattacked with flamethrowers.

It is strange to think that along the same winding Western Front where my grandfather slept on the ground wrapped in an army blanket, men like Ernest Hemingway, John Dos Passos, Robert Graves, and C. S. Lewis were also deployed. Lewis had left Oxford as a student to join the war. Hemingway worked for the Italian army in the ambulance corps; Dos Passos had a similar job with the French army. Graves, another Oxford student, was badly wounded at the Front. But though they were on the same side and spoke roughly the same language, they were from a different world than my grandfather, who had never even been out of the state of Texas before. They were men of books and a kind of learning that comes only with money and leisure and time for reflection. My grandfather never went to Africa afterward to hunt lions like Hemingway or to Majorca to write poetry like Graves. He never got involved in radical politics like Dos Passos. And he certainly never exercised his mind on hard, knobbly questions about God like Lewis. God was the dark, brooding, unpredictable presence whose arbitrary hand wrote names on bullets. If you survived the war, it was because "they weren't ready for you over there yet."

I went with him once, on another Armistice Day a few years ago when Granny was still alive, to a meeting of the Veterans of World War I. Twenty-five years earlier there had been eighty-six members of Barracks 2149. Now only my grandfather was left. They still met once a month, though, because the Women's Auxiliary had a good supply of widows left. Out in the white sandy driveway of the old frame farmhouse where they gathered for their Armistice Day meeting, my grandfather's lone red pickup was surrounded by the carefully preserved sedans of the widows. In the chickenyard behind the house, a solitary gamecock slept on a stump while several Rhode Island Red and dominicker hens scratched single-mindedly around him in the dust.

The speaker that day was a big man in a blue suit with sandy hair and freckles that ran together across his hands and face. He was a retired major who had been a liaison officer with the Turkish Air Force. His son was running for county attorney, and he knew he was speaking to people who would be at the polls in the next election.

He began by reminding us of the original Armistice Day, meant to honor both the veterans and the dead of World War I—a group, he said, no one had ever properly appreciated. There was a murmur of assent from the widows.

"But wars aren't all bad, you know. 'Course, I know and you know that some of them soldiers that laid down their lives wouldn't never of gotten to seen some of the parts of the world that they did any other way. France and It'ly and all them faraway places."

My grandfather, staring with unfocused eyes at a bouquet of plastic chrysanthemums on the coffee table, gave no sign of either agreeing with or objecting to this.

"Now I'm not for sure," the speaker said as he smoothed his shirt front with one mottled hand, "that Turkey's exactly the place I would of chosen to go myself if the Air Force hadn't of insisted on it." He grinned and waited for the widows to chuckle, but they only stared solemnly, this being Armistice Day.

He frowned and cleared his throat. "Now your average Turk I found to be a real arrogant type of a person. I don't know how many of you are familiar with Turkish history, but let me tell you, it's plenty full of blood and gore. Western Turkey is one of the oldest inhabited regions in the world. They went through your Hittites, your Persians, your Romans. . ."—here he paused and looked down at a scrap of lined paper he had palmed— ". . . clean up to your Ottoman Empire."

The last four hundred years of Greco-Turkish history he interlarded with accounts of the intestinal disorders his wife had suffered from the unfamiliar food and water during their sojourn there. In fact, he said, his family had moved a total of forty-seven times during his service career. The widows shook their heads in

pity and awe; that was the kind of detail that seemed fitting for
Armistice Day.

"Now I brought along some Turkish artifacts to pass
around here," he said, opening a cardboard box full of excelsior.
He pulled out an intricately painted coffee cup and handed it to
one of the women. "I don't know what kind of pigment it is that
they use, but I can promise you that a hundred years from now
that design will be just as bright and unfaded as it is today." She
nodded and handed it on to the next woman.

When he'd finished unpacking all his artifacts and while
the ladies were still passing each piece back and forth, he dusted
off his hands and straightened up for his finale. "What I come
here to say to you today, though, isn't just a travelogue. In fact,
I think we can learn a lesson here if we just look for it."

He frowned and clasped his freckled hands in rhythmic
little jerks. "All seven of them churches mentioned in the book
of Revelation were in what is now modern-day Turkey. That's
what's called Asia Minor in the Bible. But only two of those
churches, Smyrna and Philadelphia, have survived. Just like it
prophesies they will in Revelation: 'Because thou hast kept the
word of my patience, I also will keep thee from the hour of
temptation, which shall come upon all the world.' And those two
churches are still there today. Just like the Bible says. And the
rest of them seven churches is nothing but ruins."

"My, my," the widows murmured gently and shook their
heads. "I don't reckon you have a postcard you could show us of
them churches?" one of them asked apologetically.

"No ma'am. I'm sorry I don't. 'Course you understand it
don't necessarily look like one of ours."

All this time my grandfather continued to study a min-
iature replica of a spinning wheel with a lamp built into it.

The next lesson the speaker had for us was that there are
good people and bad people the world over. "We should judge
people as individuals, not as black or white or red or yellow or
slanty-eyed. Because in heaven we won't have these kind of
bodies nohow. We'll have a whole different kind of a body, one

that you can't tell if it's black or white." A fine dew had arisen on the speaker's florid forehead from this moral exertion. One of the widows coughed encouragingly.

"Well, now, if there's any questions . . ." He spread out his hands toward them, indicating his willingness to answer, but they only smiled and nodded and told him it had all been real interesting. "We sure do thank you for coming," the hostess said.

He collected his artifacts, packed them back into the excelsior, and said good-bye and thank you. My grandfather, as the official veteran, stood up and shook his hand.

When they heard the speaker's motor finally start outside, the hostess, a stout woman who still dyed her hair black, said, "Well, I don't see how the rich man in hell could of begged Lazarus to bring a drop of water and put it on his tongue if we don't have bodies like we're used to in heaven."

Bemused clucks rippled through the Auxiliary. My grandfather roused himself and spoke for the first time. "Well, it's this way, don't you see. The soul is the life itself. Just the pure life that's in a body, but it's got to have something to be *in*. It's like water. You don't just pour water out on the ground. That wouldn't make no sense. It's got to have a container to hold it."

The Auxiliary didn't like to contradict or even appear to question its remaining veteran. They just nodded and made little noises like doves cooing or hens settling.

"The first dead man I ever seen," he went on, "was a German soldier, not no older than I was, and I wadn't much more than a boy myself. He was sprawled up across a barbed-wire entanglement, just laying up there across it. They didn't look to be nothing wrong with him, but for this little old hole in his forehead. Just one little blue hole right here," and he pointed with his crooked finger to his own forehead. "They wadn't nothing else wrong, except for that little blue hole. But he sure was dead all right. You see, the life had gone out of him. Just spilled out there."

He sighed heavily into the silence. This was Armistice Day, and the ladies listened without interrupting. "You never

118

seen anything like them machine guns, neither," he said. "Mowed men down just like they was weeds. Clean and even as a scythe. Like mowing weeds."

———————————

IN FACT, 92 percent of World War I casualties were indeed inflicted by the awesome new machine guns. My grandfather, however, was shipped home from France in 1918 as a casualty, not of the German guns, but of a boiler that exploded along the railway behind their own lines. He landed at Newport News, got sixty dollars in back pay, his clothes, and one-cent-a-mile train-fare home to Lovelady, Texas. His discharge papers, enhanced by photographs of both President Wilson and General Pershing, hang on his bedroom wall along with a large, full-length portrait of himself in uniform, taken while he was in training at Camp Bowie.

He retains a fine sense of irony about the war. Sometimes, depending on the company and his mood, he tells the story about how he got drunk the night before he was ordered to lead a patrol into combat. "I didn't intend to be responsible for nobody else's life but my own in that war," he says, "and I knew they wouldn't have me leading no patrol in that condition." Then he laughs his crafty, old man's laugh, signifying he has outsmarted someone.

But more often he tells about what happened the day before his very first battle. "I got two letters from home that day," he says. "Of course, at the front it took some days for the mails to catch up to us there. I opened the first letter, and it said how my brother Hoyt, the one that was just older than me, how he'd come down with the Spanish flu. The next letter I opened told me he was dead."

He has a certain relish for the ironies of this dark and double-dealing God who sent the younger brother off to a bloody war and brought him safely home again while taking the older brother left at home. Such ironies do not humble him, though. They make him defiant.

Several years have passed since I went with him and Granny to that meeting of Barracks 2149 and its Auxiliary. Now it's another Armistice Day. Granny's not here anymore. She never got to be one of the widows of the Auxiliary. Another irony.

━━━━━━

MY GRANDFATHER comes stumbling toward me now over the uneven ground of the field where his brush piles have been burning all morning. He lifts his feet high to avoid the sapling stumps that he can't see.

"Now that wadn't any big adventure, was it?" he says to me.

"What?"

"Burning this here little bit of brush."

I look at him stonily. "Why? Did you want it to be?"

He stares back, startled. "No. No, a course not." He blinks at me, and I keep on staring out across the burning acre of brush piles.

"What you looking at?" he asks testily.

"I'm just keeping an eye on it."

"If you like watching smoke, you just go right ahead."

I don't say anything. I just keep up my Indian sentinel stance. I know he wants to argue about it, wants to provoke a response. He's itching for me to ask him why he did such a foolish thing as burning a dozen brush piles higher than his head on the windiest day of the year. Then he can bluster about there not being any danger and how he doesn't care what the neighbors across the road might have to say about it. I, however, am equally determined not to give him the satisfaction.

He turns and staggers off again toward one of the piles that has burned down to white ash in the center and starts dragging the outer limbs up onto the hot coals to finish burning.

"Old coot," I say under my breath.

He drops the limbs on the fire and staggers back over to me where I still stand, leaning on the rake. He's very tired, I can tell. He's been at this all morning, and his voice is husky, the way it gets when he's used up his strength.

"Come on up to the house," he says. "We can rest there."

"No thanks. I think I'll just stay here and keep an eye on this."

"Ain't no need in that. They ain't no danger in the world. Not no danger."

I shake my head. "Just the same . . ."

He stumbles off toward the house, muttering to himself.

He could have a heart attack any minute, I think as I watch him grab a stray limb and tug it up onto the flames. All right. If he kills himself, he kills himself. Obstinate, ungrateful old coot. Does he care about the trouble he's caused everyone else today? Does he care about the high wind and the danger of catching the woods or houses on fire? No. He loves it. Loves the trouble and loves the danger. This is his way of reminding God and everyone else that he's still alive. Still alive and still defiant.

I sit on a log and watch the smoke drift south, into the woods. I wonder if it reminds him of a burning battlefield from the war. World War I was the high point of my grandfather's life. Nothing before or after—not the death of his wife or children, not the Depression—nothing else ever happened to him to rival that experience. Even though it took only a little more than a year from his long life, the stories from that time are still the ones he likes to tell the most.

"War is the *strong* life; it is life *in extremis*," William James wrote in 1910, well before my grandfather went to France. "It is a sort of sacrament." Perhaps those months of soldiering come back to him so vividly now because he is, as James put it, "reluctant to see the supreme theatre of human strenuousness closed." Has there been nothing, then, not even the strenuous and threatened existence of a working man, to rival war for putting life to the test?

He loved it and hated it, the war. He loved the sense of being a part of something significant, of the grand sweep of history and of cataclysmic events shaping the world. He loved the camaraderie and the discipline he was equal to. He hallows Pershing as his hero. He is always happy when any of his grandsons joins the armed forces. That's where they *really* learn what's what, he says, meaning discipline and, hopefully, hardship, the kind of physical hardship through which he, by surviving, proved his worth to himself.

But if men love danger and hardship so, why do they rage against their own mortality? Why does it make them angry? Animals do not get angry because they die. Weeds do not whine when they are cast into the fire. Crystals dissolving under the pressure of heat do not cry "Why me?" Only human beings are outraged at their own dissolution. That is one of the strangest facts about us. That is one of the questions about my grandfather I'm trying to unravel.

I sit down on a stump to watch the smoke gradually clear from this apocalyptic battlefield. After a while my grandfather comes staggering toward me again across a weed-choked ditch, a rake in his hand. His arms and legs are splayed out to keep his balance. He is wild-eyed and staring, trying to make out who I am through the drifting smoke and haze.

But what he's really looking for, what he's been looking for since the Argonne Forest in France where he saw his first dead man, since the cemetery in Amarillo, since the grave he dug down on the river at Romayor, and every other grave he's ever stood beside, defeated by death, is the pure life that's in a body, poured out on the ground.

KORSAKOFF'S PSYCHOSIS

KORSAKOFF'S PSYCHOSIS is an organic brain disease often found in chronic alcoholics and others suffering from vitamin deficiency. It affects cells in the thalamus, that region of the brain located above the reptilian brain-stem but below the cerebral cortex and through which all incoming sensory perceptions are routed to the cortex. Although this form of amnesia allows the brain to function normally for the most part, it seems to affect the ability to form new memories, especially memories of episodes or events. People with Korsakoff's psychosis appear unable to transfer that kind of short-term memory input to long-term memory storage.

Korsakoff victims can learn and retain new skills; their store of facts and formulas used for logical reasoning seems un-impaired. They are able to drive a car normally and can success-fully work puzzles and solve math problems. However, they are unable to remember information from a conversation held less than a minute ago. In fact, the limit of their episodic memory is about twenty seconds. Beyond that, they have no recall of what has happened to them.

Since memory loss is embarrassing, they retrieve facts from their long-term semantic memory in order to weave a plausible story that can serve as a substitute for their actual recent past. Because they retain both their skill and their seman-tic memories, they are frequently able to carry off brief social encounters with no one being the wiser about their condition.

The episodic memory of a Korsakoff patient is like a ragged seine full of large holes. Unable to encode any new memories of personal experience, they live with a diminishing history in what William James called the "specious present," that portion of time we perceive as "now."

The Trip

Ask her forgiveness?
Do you but mark how this becomes the house:
"Dear daughter, I confess that I am old;
Age is unnecessary: on my knees I beg
That you'll vouchsafe me raiment, bed, and food."

—*King Lear*, II, iv

"REMEMBER?" I ask her.

"I can't remember."

"Sure you can. If I can remember it, I don't see why you can't."

"Ever since I had that spinal meningitis right after the twins were born, there's whole big blocks of things I can't remember. They're just a blank."

"But why does it always have to be something like *this* that you can't remember?"

"How should I know? Besides, I wonder if you can really remember those early things anyway. I mean, how much of it is your own memory and how much is just what you've heard older people talking about and you've heard it so many times that you only *think* you're remembering it? You know what I mean?"

"Okay then. What's the earliest thing you even think you can remember?"

"Well, I've always *thought* I could remember the hurricane at Palacios."

"But you couldn't have been more than two years old then. That was in 1942."

"See what I mean?"

"Well, go on. What do you think you remember about it?"

"I remember—or I think I remember us going out in the field behind the house and laying down between the furrows."

"Just like he always says?"

"There. See? You see what I mean?"

"Go on."

"And the wind and the rain and hanging on to the mesquite bushes."

"Because he was afraid the storm might blow the house away."

"That's what he says. Though naturally we were probably in more danger out in the field than in the house. But he always knew best about everything. He was like God or something. And he could make you believe it too."

"But it didn't blow the house away."

"No." She pauses and presses her hand against her chest, her fingers splayed as though she is keeping her heart from escaping. "But what I do remember is the fear. Just the feeling of absolute terror. Whenever I think about it today, I can still recall the fear. It comes back to me all of a sudden."

"Even though you were only two?"

"Yes. That's the only thing that makes me believe maybe I *do* remember. The feeling is so strong."

========

THAT WAS SALLY, my grandfather's youngest daughter, his last child.

As for me, I don't remember the storm at all, although I've heard about it often enough—about the carcasses of drowned cattle floating across the bay and washing over the seawall, about the wind lifting one corner of the roof up off the house and Uncle Buck and a cousin hanging onto it, holding it down so it wouldn't blow away. I don't even *think* I remember anything about the hurricane of 1942 myself, but then I'm five months younger than Sally. Maybe she had already started to talk. Maybe you can't remember until you have words.

========

"DO YOU remember the house burning down? Not in Palacios. Here."

"Oh yes. Of course I remember that. I hadn't started to school yet, and I was home alone with Mother. Daddy was out in the woods somewhere when he saw the smoke. Mother and I did what we could, just the two of us, but there wasn't much we could save. Just a few little things. Pictures, mostly."

"How did it start?"

"From the stove."

"You mean an explosion? Was it a coal-oil stove?"

"Oh no. Wood. It was a wood stove. And the stovepipe got too hot and caught the ceiling on fire. You know, where the pipe went through it." And she runs her hands over an invisible pipe in the air above her head and then flattens out a plane to indicate the ceiling around it.

"It happens a lot, I guess."

She shrugs. "I guess. We're the only people I ever remem-

126

ber it happening to though. And then afterwards people brought us stuff. Clothes and bedding and stuff. It was winter."

"Where did you live after that?"

"In the barn. Daddy fixed it up somehow. I remember the dirt floors. And how cold, bitter cold it was."

We fall silent for a moment, the past exerting its power, making a space in the present for those lights and shadows, those voices. I remember living in the barn too, the frost-flowers on the glass panes my grandfather had set into the tin walls, the smell of kerosene, the damp dirt floor.

"And after that?" I ask.

"We moved to Boswell. Out on the Four-Notch road."

"And from there to Kittrell?"

"Yes. Kittrell. They always called it a 'box house.' I don't know why."

"It's because it was made from boxing planks they used for shipping crates on the railroad. I asked someone."

"Really?"

"I liked Kittrell."

"That's because you didn't have to live there. What I remember is the three of us—Parker and Leighton and me—leaving our lunches under a log every morning on our way to catch the school bus down on the highway."

"Under a log?"

"Everybody else bought their lunch at the cafeteria, and we didn't want to be the only ones carrying our lunches. So we just left them. I don't know what we did at noon. Went without, I guess. And then we ate when we got off the bus every afternoon. We got the lunches out from under the log and ate them in the woods."

"Surely you couldn't have been the only ones who carried a lunch to school."

"Well," she lifts her shoulders and turns away. "Those others . . ."

There it is again. The same pride, the same disdain for other people's categories, instilled by their father. They do not

127

see, never have seen themselves as part of a class. None of his family would ever make common cause with any group—not Klan, not union, not party. To join a group is to dilute one's independence. One may make temporary alliances, but one's primary loyalty is always to oneself and one's blood ties. There is their family, and there is the rest of the world. Those are the only categories that make any difference. At least that's the way it used to be.

A seven-year-old girl with dark, heavy braids, already so severed from her classmates that going hungry for eight hours a day out of allegiance to her two older brothers was no great burden. She told no one, was scornful of pity, held herself apart.

None of them ever had any choice about their isolation; they never played ball, joined a team, belonged to a group. Your family was your group. You obeyed your father. You were loyal to your brothers, sensing the great gulf that separated you from other people, outsiders. You grew up thinking you and your two brothers would always live together, different from everyone else, but that wouldn't matter because you would make your own world, secure from outsiders. Parker would farm, Leighton would be a doctor, and you would keep house for them.

AT LEAST that's what you used to want. I remember you saying as much the year this house was built and we raced across the floor joists.

But time is relentless. It feeds on the future, devours dreams, moves like a swarm of locusts over the fields of hope.

Leighton died. Parker went to war and through three wives. They left you alone with outsiders. Who was left for you to belong to? What were you supposed to do? Stay home with the two old people the rest of your life? Can anyone blame you for your diminishing allegiance to blood? Weren't you the youngest, after all, the one they left behind?

Blood-betrayed, you've become, quite understandably, a modern person, one who has no need of the past. One disposes of the past by killing memory. And when it is dead, the people who inhabit that past can't haunt you anymore.

Maybe it was harder on you than the rest, having been born into the modern world, yet having to live in it like a leftover oddity from another age. Even though you were the last, the baby of the family, the apple of his eye, and thus privileged beyond all your brothers and sisters, no doubt you felt the contrarities, the differences between yourself and outsiders more keenly than the others. When they were growing up in the thirties, many people were poor and lived on farms. All children carried their lunch to school, if indeed they got to go at all. But by the fifties, life had changed. No one expected to be poor anymore.

======

I REMEMBER the trip we took that summer when we were both thirteen. Your father and mother sat side by side in the back seat of Rachel's car all the way to Omaha, as though they were sitting on a bench at a train station, just the two of them among strangers, their feet together and their hands folded on their knees. When we stopped at cafes along the way to eat hamburgers, the two of us delirious with novelty, they sat in the car, still waiting for the train.

When we got to his son's house, it was no better. The two of them sat on the furniture in the living room as though they were in a doctor's waiting room. Uneasy at being indoors for so long at a time, your father got up abruptly and went out for a walk, through the maze of suburban sidewalks. He was gone a long time.

"Daddy, did you get lost?" Rachel asked when he finally returned. He didn't answer her. He was ready to go home the next day.

Rachel took us to the Blackstone Hotel downtown for

lunch. Do you remember? They wouldn't go, of course, and we were secretly relieved. We wanted to be able to take in the huge starched napkins, the pale pink flowers, the enormous black menu with a gold tassel. We wanted to be able to shift the heavy-handled knives on the expanse of tablecloth and stare and stare, without them sitting there like immutable monoliths, impervious to the effects of elegance.

Had your allegiance already begun to shift?

"We can eat dinner right here," he had said. "They ain't no need in going to no hotel to eat dinner."

"It's not just a matter of eating," Rachel said. "I want Sally to see a little of the outside world, Daddy. Something different."

He didn't reply. What could he say? The world was there. It wasn't a world he understood. He didn't like it, but he couldn't keep it from you. Just like all the others, you would be lost to it too.

Later that night, sprawled across the bed down in the basement bedroom, we talked about what we would do, where we would go, someday.

"I'm never going to get married," I said. "I mean, look at Aunt Marilyn here. She's got four kids. What does she do? Laundry. Housework and laundry." I already took for granted a world of washing machines and vacuum cleaners. "I'm not going to be stuck with that the rest of my life." I had visions of myself living perpetually in a replica of the Blackstone Hotel, only in New York or Paris instead of Omaha.

"But she must be happy," you protested. Aunt Marilyn wore Bermuda shorts and kicked off her sandals as she tucked her feet up under her on the sofa. The very casualness with which she treated the wonders of her world—that was what seemed so desirable to you. For her, life was not fierce or guarded. One padded from room to room across wall-to-wall carpet, easy, familiar with comfort. One worried about braces for the children, or getting a suit back from the cleaners in time. Easy, comfortable worries that could belong to anyone. It meant you belonged to the world, the outside world, where your worries were the same as other people's. Where you weren't hemmed in by dark, looming trees and stretches of wet, plowed fields.

"Happy?" I said. "You call that happy? Watching television and taking out the trash?"

"But she is," you insisted. "She must be."

I yawned. If suburban housewives were happy, I supposed they deserved it.

"I'll prove it," you said suddenly. "I'll go ask her!" And before I could sit up and stop you, you were up the stairs. I heard you repeating breathlessly to the grown-ups, "Ginger says . . ."

I could have died.

———

"How did the trip go?" my mother asked when Sally and their father got off the plane. They were the last ones off. He had come staggering down the tunnel after all the other passengers had hurried away, Sally slightly behind and to his left.

"He wouldn't let me get a wheelchair for him," she said, just below his range of hearing. "He's been terrible. You wouldn't believe."

"Hello, Dad. Did you have a good time?" my mother asked again.

"I will never, ever try this again," Sally said, rolling her eyes heavenward.

"Do you want to sit down here and rest a minute before we go get your luggage, Dad?"

"God, I hope they got it on the plane at Dallas. You wouldn't believe. You know what that terminal is like, and we had to walk, *walk* from one concourse to another to make our connection. And he refused to ride in a wheelchair. In fact, he got real ugly about it. I just knew we were going to miss our plane. I tell you—it's worse than traveling with a three-year-old."

"You wait here, Dad. We're going to get the luggage. We'll be right back. We'll just be around the corner."

"Rachel and Sam—" Sally stopped in mid-sentence as she pushed through the turnstile, scanning the carousel for her bag.

"How are they?"

"Fine, so far as I can tell. Rachel still can't get around too well, but she manages. Of course, there wasn't much to do there. Daddy went out with Sam a couple of times. But mostly I more or less just visited with Rachel."

"That must have been nice. Is that your bag there?"

"I think so. But he gets so disoriented. I was absolutely frustrated. He had to get up in the middle of the night, all right? And I guess he forgot where he was or something. He was off in that little bedroom next to Rachel's. He must have waked her up because she called to me—I was sound asleep, of course. She can't get up very fast, you know, she's still using that walker. So I had to get up and go find him. He was wandering around in the dark, trying to find the bathroom. I don't think he even knew who I was at first. And by the time I finally got him there, well, you wouldn't believe. He had already just messed all over himself. I liked to threw up. It was terrible. So I had to try to clean him up as best I could, and the bathroom too. It was awful."

"This one too?"

"Yes, that burgundy one. And then I went in to check his bed the next morning, and sure enough, the sheets were all messed up too. So I had to strip the bed. It's just been a nightmare."

"And this one's Daddy's."

"I think so. I don't know why he had to take that big old thing. It was just for the weekend."

"Here we are, Dad. You ready?"

"Say, you don't mind if I rush on, do you? I have someone waiting for me. We have tickets to the symphony this afternoon. I'll be up to see you again when I get caught up at the office. Bye now, Dad." She brushed a kiss on the side of his forehead as she turned away, rummaging for her keys.

My mother had her father wait on the sidewalk while she

went to get the car out of the parking lot. She was almost running because she was afraid he might wander away or step off the sidewalk in front of a taxi. But he was still there, blinking like a bewildered child at the airport traffic as she pulled up beside him and hurried around to open the door on the passenger's side. He got in in his usual way, folding himself up a piece at a time and then dropping suddenly onto the seat.

"Let's go home," he said. He even smiled at her broadly. "I sure am proud to see you."

=====

I *THINK* I remember that Marilyn said that, yes, she was happy. I was too embarrassed to listen to the answer. I could hear all the grown-ups laughing upstairs.

"See?" you said when you came back downstairs, your eyes glowing with triumph. You wouldn't have said that unless she had told you she was happy.

I didn't see how I could ever come out of that basement again. It was the first thing I thought of when I heard she had died of cancer about ten years later.

=====

"SALLY CALLED. She said her and what's-his-name would be up later today. She said she'd leave the office early in order to miss the traffic."

"Coming to see *Daddy?*"

"I *presumed* that's what she meant, but she didn't say. All I did was take the message."

"But I don't have anything to fix for dinner and we have church tonight."

My father gave his so-what-do-you-expect-me-to-do-about-it shrug and kept working on his crossword puzzle.

133

"Well, did she say they were coming for dinner?" my mother asked, her hands on her hips.

"Honey, she said just exactly what I just told you she said." He put the paper down and sighed.

"Well, what am I supposed to do—" She threw up her hands and then ran them through her hair.

He got up and went out, shaking his head and muttering to himself.

"She had a dream," my mother said when she called me later that night. I could tell she was excited.

"What?"

"She dreamed that Daddy had died."

"Oh."

"That's why she came up, you see. She said it was just so real that she couldn't get it out of her mind."

"The dream?"

"Yes. And she said she realized how ugly she had treated him that time she took him up to see Rachel in October. She said she wanted to apologize to him for that."

"Did he remember?"

"Who knows?"

"I mean the trip. Did he even remember the trip?"

"Probably not. Tomorrow he probably won't even remember that she's been here."

"No. Probably not."

"But at least she tried. I mean, it was all she could do, under the circumstances."

"Yes," I said. "It was all she could do."

LEAR

EDWIN MUIR, the Scottish poet and critic, delivered the following as part of the seventh W. P. Ker Memorial Lecture at the University of Glasgow in 1946:

Of the tragedies *King Lear* is the only one in which two ideas of society are directly confronted, and the old generation and the new are set face to face, each assured of its own right to power. Regan, Goneril and Cornwall never feel they have done wrong, and this is because they represent a new idea; and new ideas, like everything new, bring with them their own kind of innocence. . . . To Goneril and Regan, Lear is hardly even a father, but merely an old man who thinks and feels in a way they cannot understand, and is a burden to them. He, the representative of the old, is confronted with something brand new; he cannot understand it, and it does not even care to understand him.

There is something more, then, than ingratitude in the reaction of Lear's daughters, though the ingratitude, that "marble-hearted fiend," strikes the most deeply into his heart. This something more is their attitude toward power, which is grounded on their attitude to life. It is this, more than the ingratitude, that estranges Lear from them. His appeals cannot reach them, but, worse still, his mind cannot understand them, no matter how hard he tries. As this attitude of his daughters violates all his ideas of the nature of things, it seems to him against nature, so that he can only cry out against them as "unnatural hags." "Unnatural" is the nearest he can come to a definition of the unbridgeable distance that divides him from them; his real struggle is to annihilate that distance, but

135

he never succeeds; in his most intimate conflict with them he never comes any closer to them. When Regan shuts him out in the storm her action is symbolical as well as practical. His daughters are inside; he is outside. They are in two different worlds. . . .

Lear is very old, almost Saturnian in his legendary age; the kingdom in him exists as a memory and no longer as a fact; the old order lies in ruin, and the new is not an order. The communal tradition, filled with memory, has been smashed by an individualism that exists in its perpetual shallow present.

Edwin Muir was himself the son of a tenant farmer in Orkney, where he lived until he was fourteen, when his family was evicted from the farm and forced to move to the Glasgow slums. Much of the imagery in Muir's poetry is rooted in the landscapes of his childhood.

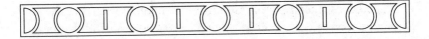

The Road

THE ROAD to Palestine runs straight north from Trinity. The old man knows this, and when we turn west at the Trinity post office onto what is now Farm Road 230, he speaks up.

"This ain't the road," he says.

"Ginger wanted to come this way, Daddy," the woman driving says. "She remembers when you used to live out this way at Kittrell."

He doesn't say anything, but he bunches up his shoulders inside his fresh khaki shirt as though resigning himself to a long trial of his patience and stares out the window on the passenger side. "Broyles Chapel," he had told her when she had asked him where he'd like to go for a drive. "Up around Palestine where I was a boy."

It is a fine morning to drive along the backroads, seeing how things have changed. Forty years ago the roads were dirt and the woods were thicker. Every fingerling creek had to be crossed on a rattling wooden bridge then. I had been afraid of bridges when I was six years old, and I had sat in the back seat of our Ford with my little brother, anticipating each one with a terrible and delicious dread.

Today, though, the creeks run through concrete culverts and you glide over them, not even noticing when you cross one.

137

In May now the weeds are already high along the asphalt. The trees make tunnels over the road with their arched branches, except for those stretches where the land has been cleared for fields.

About eight miles out from Trinity, the woman says, "There. That's it." She slows down and points to an old gray ghost of a church building, a wooden box with double doors set square in the front and a row of windows down both sides.

"Daddy helped to put that steeple on, didn't you, Daddy?"

The old man turns and then looks out his window again, away from the church. The building, long abandoned and leaning, recedes behind the car like a dream fading from memory even as you try to recall it.

"That's it?" I ask, disappointed. "That was Kittrell?"

"The church building was about all there ever was to Kittrell," she says. "They only called it that after a doctor who lived there. The same doctor that treated Sam Houston when he got pneumonia and died."

"Well, then."

About a mile farther we pass a dirt road off to the right. "Remember, Gin? That was the road to the house."

I don't remember. It is marked with a green county road sign now that says "Bo Brown Road." I have no idea who Bo Brown is. What I would like is to turn off the highway there and ease down the dirt road, going slow so as not to stir up the dust or rake the bottom of the big Pontiac on the hump between the tire ruts. I would like to find the old unpainted farmhouse where my grandfather grew his last cotton and sorghum on the shares.

I recall the high, empty, rough spaces of the house, the barn and the corncrib, the immense warm animals that terrified me. The magnificent isolation of the place, cut off from the road by the dense woods hung with ragged, melancholy Spanish moss, made it appear to brood in a kind of primeval potency. In my eyes, my two young uncles and Sally lived the life of Robinson Crusoe or Peter Pan's Lost Boys. They shot squirrels from oak trees and ate them for supper. Their muscled hands stripped milk, still smoking, from cows' bodies, and shot it in hard, needlelike streams into echoing buckets.

But they didn't feel like characters in books they had never even read. They were restless in this grand, shabby Eden made up of space and silence and trees. And for my grandfather's wife, submerged in the silent lake of her own dark memories, it was a place of judgment and punishment.

Only for my grandfather was it escape from a world changing too fast. It didn't matter to him that they owned no automobile, wore homemade clothes, and never got to go to the picture show on Saturday afternoon. That was the kind of life he had always lived. And being poor and isolated seemed a small price to pay for being left alone to raise his crops and his family in his own way.

"What do you remember most about Kittrell, Daddy?" my mother asks.

"Old man Maddox. The one that died while I was with him. While I was holding him right in my arms. Took a dose of soda, thinking he had indigestion, but it turned out it was his heart. Died just like that. Right in my arms." He pauses. "Why did we take this road anyhow?" he asks querulously.

Farther west, at Eastham, the state prison farm, the road makes a ninety-degree turn and angles north again. The fields are emerald green. They sweep away in elegant combed rows toward the river.

"This is the best farmland in Texas," the old man says. "A feller could feed himself and his family forever, just sitting here. That Trinity riverbottom, that's where I first went to herding convicts. That's what I was a-doing when I married your mother." He turns away. "I never have liked this country too well ever since then."

Another ten miles north, at Lovelady, the farm road rejoins the main highway. The railroad runs through this town, though of course it doesn't stop here anymore and the depot is deserted now. In 1918 his father and mother watched every day for the train to come in, waiting for their son to return from the war. They were to hang out a white sheet on the front porch when he arrived so that all the neighbors, including his married sisters and brothers, would know he was back.

Next to the tracks is a cotton gin where the year's crop from the riverbottom used to be loaded onto the train for shipping to mills in Houston. Now the gin is rusted and overgrown with honeysuckle.

"I worked at that gin," he volunteers as we edge up and over the tracks.

"What did you do?"

"Tied the cotton out," he says, "and loaded it wherever it was they wanted it till the train came to carry it off to the mill."

"Weren't you born in Lovelady?" I ask my mother from the backseat.

"In Wooters, really, a couple of miles east. But there's not a road that goes there anymore."

"They was a coal mine there," my grandfather speaks up suddenly. "I was working there, unloading coal cars, when you was born. The coal'd come up out of the ground, and I'd open up that tipple, I think it was they called it, and the coal would fall out and into the coal car."

"Did you ever work down in the mine?"

"Underground?" he says. "No ma'am. Oh, I been down in there. Just to satisfy my curiosity, you might say. But I never was no miner." The way he says it, you know that being a miner has some taint attached to it in his mind.

I don't know what "tying out cotton" means, and I don't understand just how the coal was brought up from underground or what a tipple is, and I don't intend to ask him. He hates having to explain things, and my mother and I are trying to keep him in a good mood for the rest of the day's outing.

When we finally reach Palestine, it is still not yet ten o'clock. "Not too soon," he says. "Don't go around on this here loop now," he instructs his daughter, waving away the convergence of the east and west highways with his bent hand. "Just go on straight into town on the main road." His fingers drum on the dashboard until he's satisfied that she is following his instructions.

"Came up here once on that senior-citizen bus with them old people," he says, suddenly jocular. "To see the dogwood blooming, they said. Like they wadn't plenty a dogwood in the woods all around them where they live. Drove a hundred miles to see dogwood." He shakes his head. "Must not a-knowed where they was going, either. Just stayed on that loop. Went right around the town."

We head straight for the center of town, though, the courthouse of Anderson County. "Just stop at any filling station," he tells her, his hands twitching nervously. "They'll know me here."

"Dad. You haven't lived here in seventy-five years."

"They'll *know* me, I tell you."

We circle the courthouse, a quasi-Georgian sprawl with a native pecan tree planted in every corner, and pull into a parking place.

"You ain't stopping here, are you?" he asks incredulously. "We don't owe no taxes in *this* county."

"Ginger wants to see it, Daddy. She's interested in old courthouses."

"Come on," I say as I crawl out of the back seat and open his door. "Maybe you'll run into somebody you know."

He gets out of the front seat without replying and blinks in the bright mid-morning sun. This is not the courthouse he remembers. That one burned down seventy years ago.

We go in the east side, marked as the main entrance by the strip of green indoor-outdoor carpet on the steps. Inside, the center of the building is cored by a spiral staircase with wrought-iron railings running up three flights. Above the gray marble wainscoting hang the portraits of past county judges. At the west entrance a wire rack is filled with pamphlets from the Baptists and the Christian Scientists and copies of *The Plain Truth* magazine.

A woman with tight black curls comes out of an office, clipping across the marble floor in high heels.

"Excuse me, ma'am," my grandfather says, "can you tell us how to get to the West Point Tap Road? That's what we're a-looking for."

"Well," she peers at him doubtfully a moment and then turns to my mother. "You go out Jackson here," she points north, "and when you get to the loop, you follow that around, oh, about a mile. There'll be an exit."

"My father used to live here," my mother says by way of explanation.

"My daddy had a store on the north side of town," he adds. "Name of Adams? My brother Alver worked at the salt-works, and my brother Dick drove a transfer wagon down at the depot. And I kept up the park grounds too. You see, I had a family to support then." He does not ordinarily volunteer so much information to strangers, and it has taken the breath out of him.

"Is that so?" The woman nods and smiles brightly at him. "Well. Just make yourself at home, sir. Of course, you'll probably find things have changed a little, you know." She winks at my mother and disappears through another door with a frosted-glass window.

We climb back into the car, and my mother pulls out onto Jackson Street and finds the loop.

"This ain't the way," my grandfather keeps saying. "You oughtn't to of gotten on this here loop. Don't no loop go to the West Point Tap Road."

"I'm just following the directions the lady gave us, Daddy. It's all changed since you lived here, you know."

"You just get me to the West Point Tap Road and I can find it," he says peevishly.

We pass muffler shops, fast-food chains, drive-in banks, discount stores. From the back seat I am watching closely for a street marked "West Point Tap."

"There, Mother, at the Seven-Eleven."

"What'd you go and turn there for?" he asks.

"The sign said this was the road, Daddy."

"This ain't the road," he protests. "I know the road."

"You want to argue with the signpost?" my mother says. She clenches the steering wheel more tightly.

The West Point Tap Road wanders through housing subdivisions and by a new brick junior high school. He recognizes nothing. After a stretch, the road veers west and isn't so well paved anymore. My mother is hoping to find an old frame farmhouse, something that still remains from seventy or more years ago, something he might recognize. But the farmhouses have been replaced by brick ranch-styles or mobile homes with metal sheds in back. It is impossible to orient oneself to the way it was, or must have been.

"Let's stop at a filling station and ask," he says again.

"What would you ask them?" she says in a level tone.

"Where I came from and where I'm going." He looks surprised at the portentous sound of what he's just said, and he laughs.

We're well out of town now, out into the countryside again. We pass a government installation that sends up balloons to test the weather. This is where he used to ride and hunt over the unfenced land as a boy. Around a bend in the road we come upon an old woman standing in the front yard of a brick house set well back among the trees. Chickens are scratching around her. She is staring into the distance and smiles vaguely when I wave. Does she know the same places he does, I wonder. Maybe she's been waiting here for seventy years to give us directions.

"I think we better turn around, don't you, Gin?" my mother says after several more miles. "We're going to be in the next county soon. And I haven't seen anything I recognize." My grandfather frowns fiercely out the window.

We retrace the pattern we have made through the maze of new-old roads, feeling our hopes for the day dissolve. But just before we get to the junior high school again, he calls out suddenly, as though struck with a vision. "Stop! Stop right here."

His daughter pulls the Pontiac alongside the curb in front of a house where a man is out in his yard working on a pickup.

Without a word, my grandfather gets out and makes toward him up the driveway. We sit in the car, expecting disaster. Who's going to remember the place he's asking for? How is he going to understand that no one knows what he remembers anymore?

We watch as the man wipes his hands on a rag while my grandfather talks to him. Then the man gestures and finally bends over a clipboard he pulls from the front seat of his pickup. When he straightens up, they shake hands, and the old man totters back to the car with a sheet torn from a yellow legal pad in his hand. He is smiling. It is a map to Broyles Chapel.

We set out once more, following the map faithfully, though my grandfather objects at every turn that we're getting it wrong. Sure enough, several miles farther into the post-oak woods and even farther west than we'd gone before, we come to a sign with an arrow pointing down a dip in a dirt road. The sign says "Broyles Chapel Baptist Church."

My mother edges the car off onto the dirt road and out under the oaks that surround the building. It's an old frame church, but shored up, refurbished, added to, painted recently. The original design—the dovecote steeple, the double-door entrance—is still discernible beneath the renovation efforts.

My mother turns off the engine and starts to get out, relief showing on her face. Despite our doubts, we'd reached our destination, a place her father remembers.

"What you stopping here for?" he demands. "They ain't planning on holding no meeting today, are they?"

"I thought this was the place you wanted to come." She turns, her feet already out of the car and on the ground, one hand steadying the camera around her neck and the other still grasping the yellow paper with the map drawn on it. She holds it out to him as though presenting evidence.

"This ain't it. I don't remember no church house like this." His voice is unsteady with anger.

"Well, they've fixed it up over the years, Dad. Come on, Gin. This is where your grandfather was baptized. And where he started to school. See, they used the same building for the schoolhouse during the week. Isn't that right, Daddy?"

He doesn't reply and she goes quickly, coaxingly on. "And *his* daddy, *my* grandfather, was a deacon here, wasn't he?"

The old man has folded his bent hands, one on top of the other, and laid them in his lap, a sort of official sign of noncompliance. He stares out the window away from the church.

"Come on, Dad. Why don't you get out and let me take your picture?"

"I don't want my picture took here. Ain't no need in it. And I wadn't baptized here. I was baptized in the river."

She puts her feet back in the car and pulls the door to. "All right, then. Where do you suggest we go?"

"You can go wherever you want to."

She starts the motor and pulls the car slowly out of the driveway and back up onto the pavement, then turns and heads south on the same road.

"They was a cemetery along here somewhere," he says, gesturing with his distorted hand to the right of the highway. "Seems like I remember it was along here."

About half a mile further we come to a sign that says "Broyles Chapel Cemetery. Maintained by Friends of Broyles Chapel Baptist Church. Grave Openings $100. Donations Welcome." For the first time today, he does not ask why we are stopping.

All three of us get out and wander among the graves. The ground—hard red clay—is dry and cracked and the cracks are filled with crickets. Tall crepe myrtles with gray, silky trunks line the central drive. Although several family members are buried here, he is searching for two graves in particular: one of a nephew who died when he was five years old, and the other of a neighbor he remembers—old man Harper, he calls him. We wander through the cemetery, trying to call his attention to the World War I veterans who would have been his age, boys he might have known when he lived here as a child. He ignores us, doing his own looking, walking among the graves with his old man's spraddle-legged gait to keep his balance on the uneven ground.

Every now and then he stops to lean on a headstone and catch his breath. Every time he stops he eyes the headstone and its message impatiently. When his daughter calls his attention to a name he might recognize, he looks away, as though he's afraid the dead might presume upon his acquaintance. The latest body, buried only a month, lies under a high mound of red dirt, looking like an obstinate sleeper who's pulled the blankets over his head.

"Look, Daddy. Here's Uncle Rudolph." My mother is pointing to one of those dual headstones that serve both a husband and a wife and look like the headboard of a double bed. On many such headstones in this cemetery, the wife's name and birthdate have already been engraved, while the date of death remains blank and pending. For several of them, dutiful children have also provided a small footstone saying simply "Mother" and have propped it against the headstone, near at hand for the final necessity.

"Rudolph? Yes." My grandfather leans close to look at the names, unable to ignore the claims of blood. "Wilma," he reads. "She dead too?"

"No, Dad. Remember I took you to see her last month."

"Yes. Sure I remember." He turns quickly away.

What is he looking for among these graves? Why did he want to come here of all places today? Every few weeks he takes it into his head to visit some cemetery, usually the one in town where his mother, his second wife, and two of his children are buried. Visiting graves is one of those strange anomalies in the modern world, inexplicable as an appendix, almost neolithic. We find ourselves suddenly standing among graves and wonder why we're there. We have a slight, sudden sense of anticipation, as though we were about to discover something, something that will act as a souvenir at least, a remembrancer, an indication, but nothing turns up; nothing happens. The more sensible or spir-itual always mention as they leave, in order to veil their disappointment, that, of course, their loved one is not really there and they never expected them to be.

But that's a lie. We do. At the very least we expect some scent, some wink, some sign. A tug on those ties to our past that will tell us it is not really lost but only lies like a wily fish down deep in the water where it can't be seen from the surface.

"Is this it?" his daughter calls. "T. A. Harper?"

He staggers toward her and stares at the headstone. Yes, he says, that's him, the neighbor he's been looking for. Beside that grave is another marked simply "Naomi."

"Last time I seen Naomi," he says, "she was in the hospital up in Houston."

"I guess she didn't make it," I say.

He frowns at this. Of course she made it. She made it back here.

A little farther down the row, we find the grave of Troy, his young nephew. I scratch away the lichen with a twig and read:

> Darling Troy has left us
> Left us yes forever more
> We nevermore shall meet him
> Till we reach that bright and happy shore.

"Do you remember him?" I ask my grandfather.

"No," he replies shortly, "but he was my brother's boy. Hoyt's."

Now that he's found those two graves, he's suddenly ready to go. As we get back in the car, he seems satisfied for the first time today. Maybe it's the guarantee of rest he wants, rather than the assurance of salvation. He doesn't like being badgered about God and his soul. This cemetery is a place of no more work, and that seems to suit him fine.

It's also a place of no more change. No one at the Broyles Chapel Cemetery is going anyplace. You don't have to keep up. Everyone is settled. This is a place where the past is wrapped up and whole, for good or ill. Nothing's going to change it now.

The past is his territory. He has the advantage of us here.

In a cemetery he doesn't expect to have to change or learn any more new jobs. After a lifetime of scrabbling from one job to another, making a harsh living such as a man of his means and temperament could manage for a family who have now all deserted him for their own jobs or death, Naomi and T. A. Harper and little Troy are the becalmed, immutable markers in an everflowing stream. He can count on them.

FOR THE LIVING, though, the past is never really wrapped up. For the past year I have been trying to reconstruct my grand-father's life, to gain some sense—some feel or taste—of what it was like. To understand the demands it made on him and in what ways he has or has not been equal to those demands. For what is he to be praised and in what found wanting? This is the task of commemoration, upon which whole cultures have been built. Ours isn't one of them. We don't ordinarily keep old people on display, or even out in plain view, where we can walk all around them and contemplate them from every angle, trying to figure out how they got to be the way they are and how that way holds up in the end.

Nevertheless, whatever happens to my grandfather when we bury him, there will still be reverberations of him we cannot close up within the grave.

There is another story from the time when he worked in Palestine, one he has probably forgotten. He was a young man then—and anyway, parents often pay no attention to events that stay in their children's minds forever. I learned the story from a cousin who happens to figure in it herself. It is a story that has to do with work, that indurate element that has always defined the boundaries of his life.

═══════

"SEE THERE. See? I told you so!" Three little girls—the oldest and the youngest dark-haired, and the middle one fair—stood on the steps of the pavilion, gazing across the empty expanse of wooden floor to where an upright piano sat with its sounding board turned toward the center of the space. The three took another step up.

"And I can play it," the tallest one said. "You want to hear me?"

"Should we?" the fair one hesitated. The three looked around. Outside the shade of the pavilion, the June roses were blooming, yellow and peach. The grass in the park was still green, not yet bleached by the late summer sun. But the shadowy interior of the pavilion beckoned, cool and dark. A few blocks away the log train, crossing the tracks, blew its whistle. Their bare feet took another step up. They stood and looked at the piano, solid in the shadows.

Suddenly the youngest girl ran up the remaining steps to the pavilion floor, where she turned and looked at the other two, her hands on her hips.

"I *dare* you," she said. "I double-dog dare you to do it."

The two other girls stared at one another. Then they clasped their hands together and ran up the stairs too. They advanced across the floor in a kind of holy horror. On this very floor they had seen grown people—the thought of it made them dizzy—dancing, spinning in circles of voile and crepe. Electric lights, strung on a wire along the outer edge of the pavilion, burned in the night then, and the girls would imagine that the pavilion was a ship floating by while they watched from their dark and landlocked shore. And there would be music—not just the piano, but a fiddle, and sometimes a banjo or a mandolin. The vision left their chests tight and aching.

But now, under the midday sun, the light and dark were reversed: the glare was outside and the shadows were under the

149

roof. They sensed that this was the way with magic; in the common light of day it veiled its glory. There was nothing magical, for instance, about the hot path from their house to the pavilion in the park, where the dust made soft puffs around their feet, nor about their mothers, who were sewing on the back porch at home, watching the youngest baby crawl off its pallet and talking about its teething and how they would put up tomatoes this year.

The three girls had crept away to the park together, not asking, but feeling safe in going, since the father of the two dark-haired girls was the groundskeeper there. They even thought of the pavilion as theirs now in some secret way. When they heard the music floating across the distance through the summer night or caught a glimpse of its lights flickering through the trees, there was a keen, proprietary edge to their pleasure.

The pavilion was the big surprise they had for their cousin when she came to visit, their jewel of the summer they had saved to show her. And now they stood, their bare feet on the very boards that the grown-up dancing feet had skimmed.

"Look!" cried the youngest one, and she stretched out her arms and began to spin on one bare heel. "I'm dancing."

"That ain't dancing neither," her sister said. "That's just turning in circles. You better stop it or you'll be sick."

The little one laughed sharply and staggered off in a dizzy line. The older two followed cautiously, advancing toward the piano that sat like a sleeping troll in the middle of the floor. They were still holding hands.

"Come on," said the dark one. "It'll be okay."

They crept up to the piano and ran a finger over the coat of dust that had accumulated over the week. Then, very carefully, they opened it, folding back the keyboard cover gently so as not to make a sound. The tall girl stood before the line of keys, locating herself in the sequence that stretched beyond her knowledge on either side.

"All right," she whispered, "here I go. I hope I can remember." She giggled nervously. Then she sucked in her breath and put a finger firmly down on middle C. The sound it made, the vibrations that hung in the air almost palpably, was like a miracle to their ears. They looked at one another, testing its reality in the reflection of one another's eyes.

The smaller girl stood at the end of the piano, her chin propped on the edge, and stared. "Oh, Esther," she breathed.

The tall girl at the keyboard took a deep breath and pushed the middle C key again, then another and another. Then three more in quicker cadence and, finally, two more notes which she held longer.

"There," she said. "That's it. That's what Mother taught me. I've been practicing. Want to hear it again?" Her eyes were shining. She started over, more confident this time.

"*What the Sam Hill's going on here!*" The voice sounded behind them like a trumpet. They went icy all over in an instant.

"I asked you what's going on here. What in the world do you think you're a-doing—banging on that piano thataway?"

They shrank from the man as he came toward them, silhouetted darkly against the bright sky beyond the pavilion. "Don't you know I could get fired from this job if anybody was to find you young'uns here banging on that piano? Don't you know this ain't your property? Don't you know no better than to go messing around with what don't belong to you?" The tall girl saw the raised hand and closed her eyes.

"But Uncle Grady, we weren't banging . . ." the fair one began.

"And don't you talk back to me, young lady. You may get away with that at home, but that won't go here." He slammed the piano lid shut and grabbed his older daughter by the shoulder.

"Here you are, the oldest, supposed to be looking out after the younger ones, and you're leading them into mischief. You ought to be ashamed of yourself. You want a hidin'?"

Hot tears hung on the girl's lashes. She swallowed but she couldn't speak.

"I asked you a question, young lady. And I expect an

answer." His thumb ground into the hollow of her shoulder. "You want me to take my belt off and give you a lickin'?"

"No sir," she said in a choked whisper.

"You get on home, then. I don't want to see you up here meddling with what ain't yours no more. 'Specially this piano. You got no business fooling with it."

He stood there, his chest heaving and the veins standing out on his temples, while the little girls turned and crept across the floor.

All three were trembling, but shame was scalding the heart of the tallest one. When they got to the dusty path, hot in the sun, they ran. Ran from the magic, left forever behind, ran from the music, and from the man.

LATE-LIFE DEMENTIA

FROM THE MOMENT we're born, nerve cells begin to die in our brains, never to be regenerated. This is normal. At about age fifty, the brain begins to suffer other kinds of damage also. Neurofibrillary tangles, abnormal scribbles of protein in the nerve cells, slow down or misdirect the firing of signals. Senile plaques made up of old cell debris collect to clog the system with scars. This, too, is normal, at least in the sense that entropy is normal.

One can also suffer from certain neurological disorders as one grows older. These come under the general heading of late-life dementias. They are not psychological problems but actual malfunctions of the nervous system itself. Multi-infarct dementia and Alzheimer's disease account for 90 percent of these disorders.

Multi-infarct dementia is caused by a shower of pinpoint strokes. Tiny blood vessels either rupture or are blocked, depriving an area of the brain of oxygen. The accumulated damage will eventually show up in impaired vision, loss of muscle tone, or even paralysis. Fifteen to twenty percent of all late-life dementias are of this type.

Alzheimer's disease, however, accounts for 75 percent. While it afflicts only 5 percent of people over sixty-five, one-fifth of all those over eighty are stricken with it. Twice as many women as men have Alzheimer's. In all, about four million people suffer from it. It is the fifth leading cause of death in the United States.

Senile plaque formation accelerates in an Alzheimer's patient, as do neurofibrillary tangles. The brain's chemistry becomes abnormal. The advance of the disease is ordinarily very gradual. Forgetfulness and a difficulty in finding words are the first symptoms of the disease to be noticed, usually by the patient himself. The disease progresses slowly, however, and it may be some time before others begin to notice this tendency to ramble in conversation. Lack of concentration and spatial disorientation are the next symptoms. By the time the person reaches this stage, he may have passed beyond the ability to recognize symptoms himself and may in fact deny them, though some people seem to have at least periodic insight into their situation.

In later stages of the disease, reasoning and judgment no longer function effectively. The patient may not recognize the names or even the faces of family members. As the condition worsens, he may wander from home if unsupervised, become emotionally distraught and even abusive, become incontinent, or simply withdraw and become mute. In the last stages, muscle control is lost, and the patient begins to lose weight. Many must be confined either to a wheelchair or to bed, where they frequently have to be restrained, making them more susceptible to other infections and heart dysfunctions.

Although this situation doubtless shortens the life expectancy of Alzheimer's patients, survival from onset varies usually between four and twenty years, the average being seven to ten years.

The cause of this form of dementia is thought to be genetic. However, the only way to definitely diagnose for Alzheimer's disease is by postmortem examination of the brain cells.

There is currently no cure for Alzheimer's disease, nor any way of halting its progress or predictably palliating its effects.

The Money

My child, farewell:
We'll no more meet, no more see one another:
But yet thou art my flesh, my blood, my daughter;
Or rather a disease that's in my flesh,
Which I must needs call mine.

—*King Lear*, II, iv

IN MIDSUMMER the road between my house and my grand-father's gets dry and dusty. Cars and trucks passing on the road kick up a cloud of fine red grit that settles over you like a flannel sheet. People who live on our road know this and usually drive at a snail's pace in order to keep the dust down if they come upon someone on foot. I could hear the vehicle behind me bottoming out on its springs every time it hit a bump, but it was going so slow that I figured it must be driven by one of the neighbors. When it caught up with me, I saw I was wrong. It was my Aunt Irene.

She was in her van, a big blue box gutted of its once-customized interior. One of the back windows had been shattered, making a shimmering star pattern in the glass. No one

155

had asked her how it happened. With Irene, it was often better not to know.

She pulled up beside me, just inching the van along. The radio was turned up to full volume. "Hey, stranger," she called out. "You hear that?"

I could barely hear her over the racket of the radio.

"What?" I came over to the van.

"Do you wanna go to heaven?" she called out, pointing at a speaker anchored to the van roof with an oversized Twist-'em. She was singing along with the country-western tune, dragging out the words and rolling her head upward toward the speaker every time she got to the part about going to heaven. She was drunk.

My Aunt Irene wants life to be happy. She wants people to be happy. And she wants it to be easy for them to be happy. She's disappointed when it doesn't turn out that way. And when she's disappointed, she gets drunk.

None of us knows what to do when she comes home to see her father in this condition, just as nobody knows what to say to her on the telephone when she calls at two in the morning, either crying or cursing. Well, maybe we know what to say, or what everybody tells us we ought to say, or not say, but none of her brothers or sisters, so far as I know, have ever brought themselves to do or say those things. Instead, they hang on the other end of the line like a fish that's been hooked and can't get loose. Their answers tend to be short and stiff and noncommittal, but they never hang up. I don't know why this is so, but having been on the end of the line a couple of times myself, I know how trapped you feel, as though you were party to some masquerade from which you can't quite disentangle yourself. You long to escape. But hanging up the telephone—these are always long-distance calls—that would be abandonment.

Why Irene turned out the way she did has always been a reliable topic of conversation in the family. Every time she gets herself in another jam, the story gets retold—about how she ran away from home to marry Jeff only six weeks before she would have graduated from high school. And how that started the unstable stone rolling downhill.

Some blame her problems on her mother dying when she was only a few months old, and on the way she was passed back and forth for the next few years between her father and her Aunt May.

"Aunt May should have kept her," my mother says. "She even said so herself before she died. She blamed herself for not having stood up to Daddy and insisting that Irene stay with her. Irene never knew who she belonged to. That's what made her the way she is today."

Others say it was her stepmother. "She was awful hard on Irene," they'll say. "It didn't seem like Irene could do anything to please her. And then after she got older, of course, she gave up *trying* to please her. Or anybody except herself, seems like."

Whatever the cause, when she was eighteen Irene eloped with a man ten years older than she was who'd just come home from the navy.

"He just fell head over heels for her. She was an awful cute kid. Sort of tomboyish and reckless, though."

"Here she was, eighteen years old, and her daddy thought he could just forbid her to see Jeff and she'd do what he said. He should have known better. She never had been too manageable. She always defied anybody who tried to tell her what to do. Just like him."

"She just didn't come home from school one day. They had it all made up between them. Jeff picked her up, and they were off before anybody at home knew about it. Anybody except Parker. Everybody always figured she'd told Parker what she was going to do and where she would be, but she'd sworn him to secrecy. Daddy whipped him to within an inch of his life, but he never told. He was just a kid, just starting high school himself, but he never opened his mouth."

"We were all scared of what Daddy might do when he found them. He was beside himself, in a rage. We were afraid he might kill Jeff or something. But Aunt May got a hold of him and

157

managed to talk some sense into him. It wasn't too long before Jeff and Irene showed up at her house. Irene wanted to make it up with her daddy as soon as she could. She came over and walked through the kitchen door, and the two of them just stood there and looked at each other for a long time. Then everything went on like before. I guess he figured there wasn't anything he could do about it by then. The harm was already done. Everybody was just going to have to make the best of it."

For one thing, it was true that my grandfather always felt vaguely uneasy about Irene. He never would have admitted it, but he probably felt he had vacillated too long about what to do with her. She was only an infant when her mother died, and even he could see that she was better off with his sister, but it went against his grain to hand over any portion of his autonomy to anyone else, even his closest kin. And when he married again, he made a point of not intervening in his new wife's dealings with the children, however bad the situation got. He's always been a man to stick stubbornly to principles, no matter what damage it does to himself or others.

But in Irene he had a daughter just as stubborn as himself.

Lots of people in the family had "drinking problems" then. But before Irene they had always been men, which somehow didn't seem so bad. Some of them died early, sometimes by their own hand, and thereupon entered a kind of clan-Valhalla of mysterious figures tinged with ironic melancholy.

Even my Great-grandfather Silas, who was a deacon in the Baptist church, was known to take too much toddy every once in a while. "It's in the Adams blood," one of my older cousins tells me. "It only took about half a pint to make his tongue all thick." (*Only* half a pint of whiskey!) "Adams blood and whiskey don't mix," she says. "It just makes them crazy. And ever one of his sons drank too." She leans forward, resting her elbow on the arm of her chair. "I don't know if you had heard this or not, but one of them went to jail for six months for making whiskey during the Depression." She sits back and sighs philosophically. "So I guess you could say that Irene come by it honest."

Whether Irene inherited her predeliction genetically or took it up as a part of her tomboy rebellion, she must have started drinking while she was still in high school. Probably she knew where her daddy kept his bottle out in the toolshed. (Her stepmother never allowed any drinking in the house.) And there would have been plenty of cousins around who had the same propensity to buy it for her. But the reins were kept pretty tight at home, and it couldn't have been till after she married Jeff that her drinking emerged into a full-blown disaster.

She had two children, but never much maternal instinct. She was more interested in being one of the boys than a mother. She hung out in bars in north Houston a lot, working-men's bars, and developed a reputation for a rough tongue. The children, a girl and a boy, weren't very old when she divorced Jeff. No one's sure just how many times she's been married since then.

You can see this is not a romantic tale of the rebel in the family kicking over the traces. Irene escaped the arbitrary restrictions of her father, all right, but when she left him, she also left behind the era that valued her particular kind of gritty stubbornness. Her escape was into a vacuum.

After marrying Jeff, she found herself in a tract house in Houston with two babies. That was no place for the defiant, swaggering daredevil she imagined herself to be. She despised the world she had escaped to. She had never had any inclination to be a matronly housewife. What she wanted was a life of adventure, but what she got was the suburbs. There was no Argonne Forest for her. Instead of the adversity of the Depression to pit herself against as her father had, there was only the fifties and its unavoidable and uninteresting affluence. Unlike her younger sister, she never felt at home in that kind of setting. She would have made a substantial outlaw in the old West. Instead, she became a drunk in the new South.

Despite her aversion to domesticity, Irene was an exceptionally fine cook and, when she set her mind to it, a hard worker. She had worked off and on at a number of good restaurants and clubs and even did small catering jobs on her own, but it wasn't until a few years ago that she was finally able to buy a shabby little clapboard cafe in Magnolia, a town on the outskirts of Houston, where she put in a barbecue pit. Being an alcoholic, she never ate much herself, but that didn't keep barbecue from being her religion. She mixed her sauce with as much care as an altar guild decants communion wine for consecration.

The flavor in barbecue comes mainly from the smoke of whatever kind of wood is used for fuel. Hickory has always been the tradition in this part of the state, where the blue haze of its smoke hangs like a canopy in the heavy Gulf air. Irene considered switching to mesquite once, a trendy innovation recently imported from West Texas. But that would be like switching from King James to some modern version of the Bible. She figured some things ought to be so familiar you don't even need to notice them.

Every morning she laid out her meat like an offering on the metal racks and damped down the coals. Then she covered it all up to do its work of transubstantiation from slabs of long-fibered muscle, parabolas of bone, and gut-encased ground fat and flesh into barbecued brisket, ribs, and sausage. Around the edges, like Abraham's first sacrifice at Mamre, she placed the chickens.

Then she sat down to wait and drink till it was done. And, as with Abraham, a thick and dread darkness sometimes came over her there. Sometimes her husband, Lon—no one in the family is sure just what number he is in a thirty-five-year succession of husbands—had to call one of her friends to come get her. "I can't have her running off the customers," he said. Actually, what he didn't like was when she tried to get the man who drove the beer truck to kiss her.

But somehow, despite all this, the barbecue always got done. And when she reached in and pulled out a slab with her long-tined fork, the aroma enveloped you like a cloud of incense, and your knees would go weak. Before she put it through the electric slicer, she took a butcher knife honed over the years to a narrow scallop and whittled off an end to see how far the smoke had penetrated. She liked the outside to be crusty, then a quarter-inch of dark brown, and finally a red zone like tender, healing flesh surrounding the taupe middle. She would offer you some from her fingers coated with crackled fat, and you knew when you tasted it that this was barbecue that had been brooded over, like creation itself.

For the first couple of years, the cafe got along all right and even built up a loyal following. Despite the steadying influence of the business, though, Irene still managed to live as close to the edge of the law as possible, being known to the sheriff's department in at least three counties in Texas and probably a few in Louisiana for DWI charges.

It is my mother's constant fear that her sister will kill someone on the highway. Once she even went so far as to have Irene committed to the state hospital to get her dried out. That might have worked, but Irene's current husband, also an alcoholic, had her released to his custody when he discovered where she was.

In some way they are shadows of one another, she and her father. They're the only ones who really wish life was still the way it used to be. And she considers herself to be the only one of his children who truly understands him. The rest of her siblings she believes to be, one way or another, only pale and weak dilutions of his vital essence. In her eyes, they have made their peace with the world the way it is—have settled down, gotten jobs, made some kind of spiritless, accommodating success of their lives. She suspects them all of scheming to have their father put away in a nursing home. She and her daddy—they are the lone holdouts, the ones who won't give in, the outlaws, standing off the modern world with their backs to the wall. At least that's the picture she paints for herself, one executed primarily in the sepia tints of Lone Star and Jack Daniels. It's one of those ironies that haunt our private history: the child who ran away from home is the one who wants to return with her father to the past, where they can be happy together again.

"Come on over and see me after while," she says now,

gripping the steering wheel to keep herself upright in the seat. The radio has started on Rockin' Sidney's "Don't Mess with My Tout-Tout." She favors Cajun stations.

"Okay," I smile and lie. She waves and eases the van on down the hill.

Part of her sympathy with her daddy includes supplying him with liquor, which he drinks till the bottle's dry. "Please don't, Irene," my mother begs her. "He's unsteady enough as it is."

But Irene won't listen to her. "Whatever my daddy wants is what I intend to get for him," she tells my mother.

I'm on my way back up the road when the van pulls alongside me again, this time headed out toward the highway. Irene's not in much better shape than when I saw her earlier, and she has my grandfather with her now.

"We're going fishing," she calls out the window to me. "You wanna come?"

I stop in the middle of the road. "Fishing?" I repeat in disbelief.

"Sure," she says. "It's hotter'n hell in that house. Daddy needs to get out of there. I asked him where he wanted to go, and he said fishing. So that's where I'm taking him. Whatever my daddy wants—idn't that right, Daddy?" She nudges him in the ribs with her elbow and laughs.

He grins vaguely.

"Just where are you going fishing?" I ask. "Did you tell Mother you were going?"

"Oh, I don't know." She waves her arm out the window. "White Rock Creek. The lake. Wherever the fish are biting. Ain't that right, Daddy?"

He chuckles and nods. He can't make out what we're saying anyway.

"Did you tell Mother what you're doing?" I repeat.

"She wadn't at home. You tell her," she says, and puts the van in gear.

I watch them roll on down the hill.

═══════

"I JUST couldn't believe it," my mother tells Sally the next day. It's Sunday, and she's whisking around the kitchen, getting the roast, the sweet potatoes, the vegetables, the gravy, the rolls, and the iced tea all to come out even and on the table for dinner. "I tell you, I was fit to be tied when I found out. Do you see them coming yet?" She looks out the window toward my grandfather's house. "Can you imagine? Taking him off in that condition? It's bad enough that she drives in that condition, but to take Daddy off like that. Why, they could have gone into a ditch somewhere and not even been found for who knows how long."

"Here they come. I see them now," Sally says. She's come up from Houston after the early service at her church. She doesn't come all that often, and having found Irene there before her hasn't put her in a good mood. She separates the blinds with a sculptured nail and watches the pair crossing the sandy field. "The blind leading the blind," she says.

"I just hope they're sober," my mother says, putting a butter dish at each end of the table.

It appears, as we gather around the table, that they are, or at least that my grandfather is, though rather badly hung over. He has a scrape across his forehead, and his nose is swollen.

"My goodness, Daddy, what happened to you?" my mother asks as she pulls out the chair for him at one end of the table. "You look like you've been in a fight!"

He touches his nose gingerly with his bent forefinger and looks confused. "I guess I musta taken a fall."

My mother looks closely at Irene, who puts her cigarette case beside her on the tablecloth with a hand that's not too steady. Her henna-ed hair has been combed but still looks pretty scraggly, and she has a bruise on one cheek.

"Whew. What we got to eat here?" she asks loudly, ignoring my mother's questioning look. "I'm starved."

Yet when we actually start to eat, she hardly touches her food. Neither does my grandfather.

"Here, Daddy, don't you want some of these little cabbages?" my mother says, getting up and bringing the bowl around herself. That's what we call brussels sprouts around him—little cabbages, another one of my mother's small conspiracies. He wouldn't eat them otherwise. "You like these." She starts to put some on his plate, but he shakes his head.

"No, I don't want none of them."

"But I made them just for you, Dad. You always eat them."

"I'm not hungry."

"Well, here. Eat some of these sweet potatoes. They're good for you."

"No. I got a-plenty right here on my plate," he says, the irritation beginning to show in his voice. He puts his forearms down on the table on either side of his plate to ward off each new bowl she offers him.

"Oh, Daddy." She makes a gesture of exasperation to her sisters. "I just can't get him to eat."

"Leave him alone, Mother. For heaven's sake. He's trying to eat if you'd just leave him alone." She sits down with a sigh.

"Oh, he's just being a horse's ass," Irene says, and laughs harshly. "Ornery old coot."

Forks pause in midair, and eyes dart around the table. Sally catches her breath. My grandfather, who doesn't appear to have heard, goes on eating.

"That's what I keep telling him," Irene continues. Her voice is brassy, and it's clear she's not going to stop with that one remark.

"He's just plain old ornery and stubborn. He needs to take a bath, and he needs to get that house cleaned up down there. Maybe then he could get rid of those ants. They're ever where. I had to get up in the middle of the night last night and change the sheets. They were even in the bed. That's how come I got this knot on my head this morning," she says, fingering her scalp gingerly. "Stumbling over things in the dark."

Sally makes an inaudible remark and scrapes her chair back from the table. "I'll go put the coffee on for the dessert," she says stiffly.

"He don't want to take a bath, and he don't want to change clothes. He's just let himself get *filthy*," Irene exclaims. My mother's face is burning.

"Well, I told him I wadn't going to put up with that kind of nonsense." Irene pushes her own plate back and lights up a cigarette. "Didn't I, Daddy?"

He's gone on eating, either ignoring her or pretending to, but she's grown insistent now. "Didn't I tell you that, Daddy?"

He looks at her and goes on chewing, blinking behind his thick cataract glasses. I've never seen him in quite this position before.

"We weren't raised like that, you know. We weren't raised to be filthy."

"Irene," my mother says.

"Why, you should see that old pot of his he keeps beside his bed. And that stinking toilet. I don't think he can even hit it anymore."

My mother gets up and goes into the kitchen to serve the pie, and Sally takes up the dinner plates. "He'll let *her* talk to him like that," she mutters to my mother at the sink, "but he wouldn't put up with it from any of the rest of us. He's just afraid of his beer supply getting cut off."

"She's been drinking," my mother says. "She doesn't know what she's saying." Her first impulse is always to find an excuse for everyone, to smooth things over. Still, she's been hurt, not only by the disrespectful way her sister talks to their father, but by the implication that he's not being properly cared for.

"You know what, Esther?" Irene calls from the dining room.

"What, Irene?"

"I already called Lon and told him I won't be coming

165

home tonight. I'm going to stay up here and clean house for Daddy. That's what I told him and that's what I'm going to do."

"In fact," she says, when we are all reassembled at the table around the chocolate pie, "I told Lon I might just have to come move in with Daddy up here. He needs someone to take care of him. That's perfectly evident." She pauses and stubs out her cigarette dramatically. "Because no one's putting him in a nursing home so long as I'm alive."

No one makes any reply to this. No one ever does. If there's one thing we all know about drunks, it's that you don't try to argue with them. It's a losing proposition.

Later, at the kitchen window, Sally is watching Irene and her father make their uneven way back across the field to his house.

"Do you think Lon's kicked her out?" my mother asks.

Sally shrugs. "Move in with him, my hind ear," she says. "The only reason she'd want to move in with him is to find the money he's got hidden down there somewhere."

"She's not going to move in," my mother says. "That's all bluster. Not unless she really didn't have any place else to go." She twists a cup towel in her hands. "But I just wish . . ."

"Wish what?"

"I just wish I could stand up to her, not let her talk to Daddy like that. I wish I could say what I feel without being afraid I'd just start crying. That's so dumb. I feel so dumb."

"Well, *she's* not dumb. She's got him right where she wants him," Sally says, turning away from the window and smoothing down her chiffon skirt.

"I just wonder if I should let the rest of the kids know what's going on. I mean with Irene. I don't know what she might do. You see how they were both banged up."

"And that didn't come from stumbling around in the dark changing the sheets, either," Sally adds.

"Who knows what happened. Maybe they went off the road in the car."

"I'm wondering if they didn't get into a fight," Sally says.

"I guess anything is possible," my mother says, sadly. "And what if he should die like that?"

"Like what?" I ask.

"Drunk," she says, a word that always costs her something. "What if he should get drunk and fall off the porch or something and it kills him? I don't want him to die drunk."

═══════════

THAT WAS a year ago last summer. During the winter, Irene's business began to fail. Lon complained that she ran the customers off with her loud, brassy talk. And she certainly had bad luck or poor judgment when it came to hiring help. She would give work to almost anyone who asked for it, but the paychecks were only precariously covered at the bank. Many businesses, even large ones, were failing in Texas, and whether hers would have gone under anyway, even with better management, it's impossible to tell. She charmed operating capital out of friends for a while. When that was gone, she came to see her father.

The next month, a check made out to Irene for seven thousand dollars turned up in my grandfather's bank statement. My mother discovered it when she was balancing his checkbook for him.

"Daddy, did you loan Irene some money?"

"Irene?" he said uneasily. "I don't remember."

"Well think, Daddy. This is a lot of money."

"If it says I did on that piece of paper, then I reckon I did." Ever since the Ray Renfro incident he's been testier than ever about his financial dealings.

My grandfather's manner of handling money has been affected by history. He cashes his government checks and puts the cash in his safety deposit box out of a Depression-born distrust of the banking system. And Sally is convinced he has money hidden in the house or buried in a coffee can out in his weedy field.

He's touchy about his veteran's pension and his social security check, sensitive to suggestions that this is government welfare money. His regular expenses never exceed $200 a month because he goes to bed at dark, refuses to light his water heater, and never makes long-distance calls. He hasn't bought any clothes for years. The one area where he spends without regard to cost is food. He buys the same gallon of milk, dozen eggs, and pound of thick-sliced bacon every time he goes to town, almost every day. Whenever any of his children come to visit, he buys without question whatever they're willing to cook. He's always been this way about food.

He's been generous in lending too. When his brother went to jail for moonshining, he saw to it that his brother's family was taken care of. Any number of nieces and nephews have come to him over the years for small loans, which he has always kept confidential. Who knows how many of them were ever repaid?

But his children are another story. By and large, they have kept clear of him financially. The ties of blood they have found constraining enough without adding those of money.

Except for Irene.

The seven thousand only bought her another month, however. And when it was gone and the bank repossessed her equipment and the little house she had used for collateral, she did something no one ever expected. She went to live with Lon's children in Georgia.

Lon himself—if the tale she tells is true—has gone to Israel to open a mesquite barbecue stand, backed by Jewish entrepreneurs. Irene, however, was not a part of the package.

My grandfather never expected Irene, of all his children, to leave the state and go so far away. Everyone, in fact, was shocked by the news. She had lived in and around Houston ever since she had eloped with Jeff. She might have had a hard time sticking with husbands, but at least she seemed geographically rooted. But her options were narrowing. She wasn't a young woman anymore, and her health wasn't good. So when Lon loaded up the U-Haul with all their possessions and headed for his son's place in Georgia, she went along with him.

"Maybe the change will do her good," my mother told Sally over the phone.

"There's about as much chance of anything helping Irene as Congress has of balancing the national budget," her sister replied.

"At least she's got a job. A waitress in a country club there in Atlanta."

"A fox in a henhouse," Sally said.

My mother silently agreed.

Irene's middle-of-the-night phone calls continued. She was homesick. Her in-laws were nice to her, she said, but it wasn't the same.

My mother talked it over with her father. "What do you think, Daddy? Should we bring her back home? You know she has no place to live here anymore." She didn't have to spell out for him the fact that, if Irene came back, the only place she'd have to go was his house.

The old man frowned. He sighed heavily and smoothed the long strands of white hair back across his pink skull with his crooked hand. "I reckon not," he said after a while. "No, I don't believe that would be a good idee." The prodigal had waited too long to return.

My mother closed her eyes in relief. After all, her sister had already been through one fatted calf, and she'd be bringing the pigsty back with her if she came to live with her father now.

That was last winter.

Still, the matter continues to weigh on my grandfather's mind. He asks my mother frequently if she's heard from her little sister.

"Irene called last night, Daddy," she told him one morning. She had gone down to his house early to do some extra cleaning. Thanksgiving is next week, and Rachel, Parker, and Ward, the three of my grandfather's children who live out of state, are all coming. It will be the first time in twenty years that they'll all be back for Thanksgiving at the same time. "Actually, it was about two o'clock in the morning."

"She still over there in Florida?" he asked.

"It's not Florida, Dad. It's Georgia."

"Well, it *was* Florida," he said. He does not like to be corrected. "She must of moved on."

"Anyway," she went on, "as you can imagine, she wasn't in too good a shape, calling at that time. She was crying and quoting me stuff out of the Bible." She paused before she continued. She wanted to give that time to sink in before she went on to the next point. Her father just sat there in his old Naugahyde chair, staring straight ahead and tapping on the chair arm with his bent fingers.

"She said she wanted to come home for Thanksgiving but she didn't have the plane fare." My mother paused again, and he swung his eyes over toward her and stopped tapping his fingers.

"I told her I simply didn't have the money to send her right now." She swallowed hard and he looked away again. "I didn't know if you wanted to send her the money or not."

He still didn't say anything and she was uncertain how to go on.

"I guess so," he said finally. And he started tapping again, faster this time.

"You know you don't have to, Daddy," she said. "I just felt obligated to tell you, that's all."

He kept on staring straight ahead. She started dusting the defunct television set and rearranging the stacks of magazines, keeping one eye on him. Finally he heaved a sigh and slapped his palm down on the arm of his chair.

"No sir," he said. "I'm not a gonna do it. I couldn't do it for all them other children of mine, and I ain't a gonna do it for her. She has a husband to make her a living. If he can't take care of her, she aren't to of run off and married him. I can't help it. I just can't help it."

ECCLESIASTICUS

**Advice for children from Ecclesiasticus,
the Wisdom of Jesus Ben Sirach:**

Children, listen to me your father,
    do what I tell you, and so be safe;
for the Lord honors the father in his children,
    and upholds the rights of a mother over her sons.
Whoever respects his father is atoning for his sins,
    and he who honors his mother is like someone amassing
        a fortune.
Whoever respects his father will be happy with children
        of his own,
    and he shall be heard on the day that he prays.
Long life comes to him who honors his father,
    he who sets his mother at ease is showing obedience
        to the Lord.
    He serves his parents as he does his Lord.
Respect your father in deed as well as word,
    so that blessing may come on you from him;
since a father's blessing makes the houses of his children firm,
    while a mother's curse tears up their foundations.
Do not make a boast of disgrace overtaking your father,
    your father's disgrace reflects no honor on you;
for a man's honor derives from the respect shown to his father,
    and a mother held in dishonor is a reproach to her children.
My son, support your father in his old age,
    do not grieve him during his life.
Even if his mind should fail, show him sympathy,

do not despise him in your health and strength;
for kindness to a father shall not be forgotten
   but will serve as reparation for your sins.
In the days of your affliction it will be remembered of you,
   like frost in sunshine, your sins will melt away.
The man who deserts his father is no better than a blasphemer,
   and whoever angers his mother is accursed of the Lord.

Advice to aging fathers from the same source:

Observe that I have not toiled for myself only,
   but for all who seek instruction.
Listen to me, you princes of the people,
   leaders of the assembly, lend ear.
Neither to son nor wife, brother nor friend,
   give power over yourself during your own lifetime.
And do not give your property to anyone else,
   in case you regret it and have to ask for it back.
As long as you live and there is breath in your body,
   do not yield power over yourself to anyone;
since it is better for your children to be your suppliants,
   than for you to have to look to the generosity of your sons.
In all you do be the master,
   and do not spoil the honor that is rightly yours.
The day your life draws to a close,
   when death is approaching, is the time to distribute
     your inheritance.

The Reunion

"FIRE IS our biggest worry."

My mother is explaining, almost desperately, their father's current state to her sister Rachel, who's come from North Carolina for Thanksgiving. Rachel hasn't seen him for two years.

"Especially during the winter, with that space heater of his. He's always turning the gas off at the wall and then trying to light the pilot again himself. You can't make him understand that it has a thermostat."

Rachel only stares out the window, toward her father's house across the field.

"I went down there last week in the middle of the morning, and he was sitting at the table eating a pork chop while another one was burning on the stove. The kitchen was just full of black smoke. I said, 'My goodness, Daddy, you're letting this burn.' He said, 'I ain't done it. I didn't put that on there.' 'Well, who did then?' I said. 'I don't know,' he said, 'but I sure didn't.'" My mother pauses and then throws her hands up in the air. "You see what I'm up against?"

Her sister nods that she does.

"I thought we were going to lose him last January," my mother continues.

"I feel like I've got to let them all know," she told me last week, "even if they don't want to. They need to know. Even Rachel. Because if I don't tell them, they'll want to know later why I didn't. They never expect him to be as bad off as he is."

"Lamar went down to check on him one morning—it had been real cold the night before, the coldest night of the year—and found him with his mattress crossways on the bed and him huddled up in one corner of it. Half the blankets were dragged off the bed along with the mattress. The thermometer in the kitchen said twenty degrees. He didn't seem to know where he was or anything. I don't know what happened. He must have gotten up in the middle of the night and fallen or something. Lamar called me to come down, and I helped Daddy to get dressed. All the while he just kept sort of babbling to himself. I couldn't make out anything he was saying." She takes a deep breath and keeps going, as though afraid she won't get to finish.

"The pipes were frozen, of course. An icicle was even hanging from the faucet. I had to bring water down to make the coffee. He was too weak to eat anything, but I finally managed to get about half a cup of coffee down him. We got the living room warmed up and sat him down by the fire there. He was just exhausted. By that afternoon he was pretty much back to normal—or what's normal for him now. Except that he still didn't have any more idea about what time of day it was than the man in the moon. He goes to bed when it gets dark, you know, which is pretty early in the wintertime. Then he might get up at midnight or two o'clock and start fixing breakfast. Sometimes even now I go down there at ten in the morning and he's fixing supper."

Her sister Rachel shakes her head and looks down at her lap, where her good right hand is folded over her almost useless left one. She is sitting at the end of the table, where there's plenty of room for her walker. Sam, her husband, has to help her get her chair positioned at the table so she can use her good hand most easily.

My Aunt Rachel was always the beauty of the family. This

174

wasn't just a matter of looks. I've seen snapshots of all the sisters together, taken during those halcyon war years at their Aunt May's house on the bay; they smile into the camera with eager eyes. They are all tall and handsome. But there is something about Rachel in those pictures—a lack of guardedness, perhaps, or a palpable anticipation—that in three dimensions came alive as a promise fulfilled. I remember the excitement, even as a small child, of being around her.

She was one of those women who magnetize people wherever they go with their own inviolable sense of themselves. Her bones were fine as a bird's wing. Her abundant auburn hair swung to her shoulders in one of those artless page-boys of the forties. The world became suddenly smart and shining in her presence. How I knew all this then at the age of four I can't say, except that men and women alike turned to watch her when she entered a room, as though they had been waiting just for her.

Yet one of my first memories of Rachel was as she stood at the back door of the house in Palacios, watching the rain stream down the glass and crying. She could not have been more than eighteen then. She was at once beautiful and sad, the first tragic figure to mark my memory. That such sorrow could come upon someone so impenetrably beautiful stunned me. How could one who held the world so lightly in the palm of her hand, who shone and drew light to herself so effortlessly, ever cry about anything? How could common unhappiness find a breach in such beauty? It was the first inkling I had that the world was perhaps not such a snug place after all. If some hurt could come within the citadel of such an Eve as this, then none of us were safe.

She was the only one of my grandfather's children who, at least after she left home, could effectively stand up to him; he couldn't intimidate her or make her feel guilty. Irene had run away, his sons had deserted him, Sally later simply disengaged, but Rachel, everyone agreed, could face him down.

"Of course, it wasn't like that when I was still at home,"

she told me once. "No one dared to cross him then." But even as a child she had been allowed a certain latitude the others never had. He gave her a nickname—"Kitten"—because of the way she would crawl into his lap and nestle in the curve of his arm.

But he stopped calling her "Kitten" a long time ago.

"I don't fool myself about Daddy the way the rest of them do," she said. "I know what he is."

"What?" We were sitting on the fly deck of the yacht Sam had just bought from a Hong Kong toy manufacturer. He was having electronic navigation devices installed and following the electricians around while they worked.

"Ward's too much like him himself to really understand him," Rachel went on, ignoring my question. "And your mother and Bess—well, they just try to make excuses for him."

"He's an old man."

"He's always been the way he is now, stubborn and unreasonable. It's nothing new, nothing he got to be just by getting old."

"He had a hard life."

"Maybe so. But we did too, us kids. We were there too, don't forget. But that was never an excuse for us. I remember your mother having to go down to the saloon and lead him home by the hand. A child shouldn't have to do that. It was humiliating for her. The younger ones don't remember that kind of thing, of course."

"But you do?"

"You bet I do. Oh, I admit he could be fun. He liked playing his harmonica, and he liked hearing us play those instruments he bought us with his bonus check. But he could be mean too. Especially when he'd been drinking. And you never could disagree with him. Not under any circumstances. That just wasn't allowed. If he said black was white, you just had to nod your head and go along with him."

"Did you?"

"I learned how to adapt. How to stay out of the way. Especially after he married our stepmother. I hadn't even started to school then." She stopped and shook her head, remembering. "But after I left home—well, it gradually dawned on me I didn't have to do that anymore. What my father said was just as open to question as what anybody else said."

"But you've stayed on good terms. I remember when you brought him out here for a fishing trip."

She smiled crookedly. "It looks that way. But what you call our good terms were only because of Sam. Daddy never pays any attention to what I say, but you notice he'll listen to Sam when he won't listen to anybody else. To him, Sam is a success. Like that Mr. Dunham in Fostoria he's always talking about— the one that owned the sawmill? Daddy was always poor, and he has a poor man's fascination with money and power." She paused and picked up a paper cup of Bailey's Bristol Creme. "I hate that."

Sam's voice came up through the gangway. "Rachel, these guys are ready to put the program into the computer. You better come watch this."

She put the paper cup down. "Daddy's always made such a big deal about how independent he is. And I guess a part of him is—or was. But he's also in awe of people with money. They make him feel inferior. He's secretly afraid that people who make a lot of money must be smarter than he is. You know that saying—'If you're so smart, why ain't you rich'? In his heart of hearts, Daddy is afraid rich people must be smarter than he is."

"What about you?"

"I know better," she said. "I've learned the hard way. It's not smart that makes the difference." She went down the gangway to the bridge, where Sam was still calling for her. She never did say what it was.

About six years ago, after my grandfather wrecked his truck because he couldn't see to drive, she found the best eye surgeon on the East Coast and flew her father to the Duke Medical Center for the surgery. She stayed with him at the hospital, running interference between him and the modern medical world. The operation was a failure. His eyes had deteriorated too much to tolerate the transplanted lens.

"I'm afraid you waited too long for the operation, Mr. Adams," the surgeon told him afterward. "Ten years ago we might have had some success. Your tissue would have been more receptive."

"Get the hell out of here," my grandfather said. "I want to go home," he said to Rachel, who was standing on the other side of the bed. "I want to go home right now. It was you talked me into this. If I go blind, it's going to be your fault."

"Lie down, Daddy. If you get up now, it could ruin your eye completely. Then you'd be in worse shape than you were before. And you can forget that talk about this being my fault. I was trying to do something to help you, and you're so damned contrary you don't know how to be grateful. You're just looking for somebody to blame. There's not anybody to blame. It's not anybody's fault—not the doctor's, not mine, not even yours. That's just the way it worked out. So lie down and shut up or I'll have the nurses come in here and put you in restraints."

Things haven't been the same between them since.

Unlike my mother, Rachel rarely makes excuses for people. Perhaps more than any of her sisters, she looks at her father with the lean eye of objectivity. She remembers stories about him the others do not tell. She judges him austerely, like a disillusioned child.

Or at least she used to.

The intuition I had about her when I was a child turned out to be accurate. My Aunt Rachel indeed proved vulnerable to the hurts of the world. She may have looked like a fairy-tale princess, but she didn't live happily ever after. The heartache and the thousand natural shocks the flesh is heir to did not spare her for her beauty's sake. Yet even in the face of common sorrow and disappointment, she maintained her uncommon, upright grace. She may have been shut up in a desperate tower, but she remained a princess, even if a sad one. At sixty she could still charm little girls and grown men simply by the way she held her fork and glanced across the table.

Then one night about two years ago, her sense of herself

was suddenly changed, betrayed by a smudge of blood sticking in some stagnant backwater of her brain. She was in the hospital for months, and when she came out, it was in a wheelchair. The citadel had been violated, the walls not only breached but left in ruins. Her expressive shrugs and the elegant, nonchalant way she had of standing have been replaced by a ponderous concentration as she swings her braced leg through its halting gait.

She sits quietly now and doesn't have as much to say. The fairy-tale princess has retreated to some central keep within herself. She hates going out in public and having people stare at her.

"What *can* he do?" she asks me, picking at my mother's turkey and dressing. She's barely touched anything on her plate.

"He can play checkers," I say. "And he still beats anybody around. I don't see how someone who's losing his memory, who starts the same story over as soon as he finishes it, can still play checkers."

"I can," she says.

While the others are washing dishes and watching the football game, we pace, slowly, with her walker, up and down the driveway. She's afraid to try the walker on the soft ground of the lane that leads down to the woods.

"Bess wrote me that she wants me to pray with her that the Lord will take him before another summer like last year." She concentrates on the end of the cement driveway.

"Well," I say, "it's hard to know what's best."

"I wonder if anyone ever prayed that about me." She smiles one of her lopsided smiles and heaves her walker around for the trip back up the driveway. "Besides my own self, I mean."

I match my stride to her halting gait. "Sometimes it's hard to know what to hope for, what to pray for. People mean well." I wonder myself what all this is for, why people die inside their skin like my grandfather. But I don't say this. I feel blackmailed into banality by the flimsy aluminum walker.

"I suppose they do. Let's stop a minute," she says, and turns again to watch the winter sun staining the sky vermillion as it disappears across the road. The moon is beginning to glow a chill silver in the same sky.

"Bess is a nurse," she says. "I always wanted to be a nurse."

I nudge a dry sweetgum ball off the driveway with my shoe and look up at the moon.

"I've told Sam I want to move to the country. To that place he bought in the Ozarks. I want to be on a farm again. I haven't lived on a farm since I left home."

I look over at her sharply. "Are you sure?"

"Yes, I'm sure. I'd be happy there."

"Would Sam?"

She shrugs and points to a cardinal that flickers out of the brush along the fenceline and back in again, settling down for the night.

"I could ask Parker to come and run the place for me."

"And Jan?"

"Of course. Jan too."

"A farm is nice," I hear myself say.

"One more lap and we'll go in." She starts down the incline again.

"I worry about my mother," I say. "All this is so hard for her."

"Yes," she says. "It's terrible. You should worry."

"She can't seem to accept it. I know she drives everybody crazy, trying to make everything all right, trying to make the world come out even. It breaks her heart to see him like this. More than that. She feels like there ought to be something more she could do, something that would make it all right."

We've reached the bottom of the drive again. She pauses and contemplates the sky, now lavender, and the moon like a ghostly shell.

"Your mother's great humility," she says, "is what makes it possible for her to do what she's doing. It's easy enough to write it off to guilt, or a thousand other things. Maybe it's those too. But none of those things make it possible. Only humility can do that. It's what she's got that the rest of us don't have."

180

She hikes her walker around and starts up the drive again without stopping.

Indoors, the football game is over, and some are starting on another slice of pie. Sally is getting ready to drive back to Houston.

"My camera!" my mother says. "Where's my camera? We need to take a picture first. With everybody here."

"Except Irene," Parker says, getting up off the rug in front of the television set and stretching. "Too bad she couldn't have made it."

Sally takes her car keys out of her purse and shakes them. "Okay. One picture. But I need to get back early."

They all line up in front of the mantelpiece with Rachel and my grandfather sitting side by side in the middle and the rest grouped around them. He looks a little bewildered but is grinning in the middle of all the hubbub. Rachel lifts her chin, smiles faintly, and puts her good hand over his, the one with the crooked fingers.

"Ward, move in a little closer there." My father waves inward with his left hand, trying to crowd them all inside the lens.

The flash goes off, and they are all frozen there, the orphaned children and their father, for the last time.

THE SAN NICOLAS WOMAN

IN 1853 a fishing vessel cruising the waters of the Santa Barbara straits off the coast of California discovered by accident a lone woman on San Nicolas Island. She had been living there alone for the last eighteen years.

Mexican officials had rounded up all the remaining natives from those islands in 1835, taking them off to work on the big rancheros the new government carved out of the old Spanish mission lands. When they came to San Nicolas, however, the island farthest offshore, a storm was brewing. In their haste to get all the islanders on board the boat, they left without this woman, who had run back to the village to get her child. The boat sailed without her, and no one ever returned for her.

Her child died soon after, and the woman lived alone on the windy, fogbound island, moving from one vacant dwelling to another, occupying her departed clan's homes, made from whale ribs and jawbones and covered with skins. The sea provided her with abundant food, and she wore beautiful, warm robes made of birdskins.

When she was brought to the mainland almost two decades later, it was discovered that she had lived through the entire span of time from the coming of the first Russian sea-otter hunters to the islands to California's acquisition by the United States.

Citizens from the town of Santa Barbara, moved by the woman's long isolation and her bewilderment at her new surroundings, located a number of survivors from the offshore Indian tribes and brought them to see her. The meeting was unsuccessful, however. None of them were natives of San Nicolas. And none of them could speak or understand her language. She died soon after.

182

The Secret

O heavens,
If you do love old men, if your sweet sway
Allow obedience, if yourselves are old,
Make it your cause; send down, and take my part!

—King Lear, II, iv

SLIDELL WEEMS showed up early in January, after all the seasonal celebrations were over and we had settled down to the prospect of another year. I never was too clear about who the man was. He claimed to be a distant cousin of my mother's, but my grandfather's nieces and nephews were so prolific and scattered that I can't keep up with all the tributaries of their generations.

Slidell looked to be fiftyish and definitely down on his luck, a plight not uncommon among my mother's distant cousins. At any rate, she thought she recognized him when he showed up, coming in through the garage door as people do who know my parents' house and habits.

But in other ways he didn't seem to fit the picture of an Adams relative at all. For one thing, he wore an old trench coat that hung down below his knees and a knitted cap pulled over his ears. You don't see many native Texans dressed like that. It made him look like one of those street people, not only down on his luck, but decidedly urban.

That was something else that didn't seem to fit. What he showed up for was to ask for work, and the kind of work he offered to do was cutting down the beetle trees along the fence-line and around the old barn.

Three years ago the large stands of Texas yellow pine in the eastern part of the state were attacked by the pine bark beetle, an insect that had already ravaged the Ponderosa pine forests of Colorado and New Mexico. The beetle bores in through the thick, soft bark and sucks the sap out of the tree. The branches start to turn brown on the tips first. Ordinarily, pine trees lose their needles year round, but drop them from the back of the branch, nearest the trunk, so that the loss doesn't show up so much. If a pine tree starts to turn brown at the tips of the branches, you know it's a goner. In infected areas, whole stretches of pine forest turned brown, as though they had been sprayed with defoliant.

They weren't like other dead trees—say, oaks or sweet gum. You usually don't notice those are dead until one spring when the leaves don't come out. They stand there bare and lifeless, sometimes for years. They look pathetic or melancholy, and there is a certain brave beauty in their nakedness. But the pines just stood there in dry swatches, brittle and trashy looking.

Since a good part of East Texas is taken up by national forests which serve as timber plantations for big companies like Louisiana-Pacific, the U.S. Forest Service soon got involved in the beetle problem. At first there was a lot of wrangling about if or just how the infestation would be controlled. The let-nature-take-its-course school said that such infestations were inevitable and cyclical and that the beetles should be allowed to run their course. They would eventually hit a biological sink and die out. Others objected that since the forests were already "managed," natural laws of self-limitation did not obtain. For instance, lightning-started forest fires that might have gotten rid of weak trees weren't allowed to burn themselves out.

The timber industry, of course, backed the eradication approach, which eventually carried the day. They were for all-out war against the insects, even if it meant resorting to a scorched-earth policy. Leveling the forests to eradicate the beetles would also get rid of all the plants of no use to the pulp and paper industry and would make replanting with profitable pine seedlings easier.

At any rate, one day last year a man from the Forest Service came out to look around my folks' forty acres. He told them they would have to do something about their beetle trees— either spray them with an insecticide the Forest Service would provide or have them cut down and hauled away. The cost of the labor for either project would have to be borne by my parents as landowners. The one option they did not have was to simply let the trees stand.

The cost of spraying forty acres of pine trees would be considerable. On the other hand, sawmill operators had been after my father for years to sell them the pulpwood off his property. The profit would be small, but at least he and my mother would have no out-of-pocket expenses. Up to now, my mother had resisted all their offers because the big logging trucks tore up the land and started erosion. Now it looked as if they didn't have any choice. They'd have to contract the work out to private cutters with log trucks.

That plan lasted maybe two weeks. Hundreds of other landowners in the area had been hit with the same decree at the same time. They all had to scramble for cutters, and the people with thousand-acre spreads got the pick of the lot, those with dependable equipment and connections at the mills. People with small holdings like my folks got the marginal operators whose trucks had broken windshields and slick tires and were held together with black gunk and baling wire.

It was my father's hope to get the dead trees out during July, when you can usually count on the weather to be hot and dry, so that the truck wouldn't get bogged down in the woods. The weather cooperated, and on the days that his truck was running, the logger my parents hired was able to get a few loads out. Then the sawmills began to fill up. The mill he was selling to, which was north of town, soon had mountains of pine stacked in all its available space. It had to run sprinklers on the stacks night and day because of the fire hazard. It wasn't long before that mill quit taking any more timber—and so did all the others. The logger rolled his truck out of the woods for the last time and hocked his chain saw, leaving the big logs he'd already cut lying about in the woods like matchsticks.

The beetle war ground to a halt, at least on private property. The insects had won. Now the Forest Service was concerned only with reconstruction. In the national forests they brought in bulldozers to clear the beetle trees, pushing them over and piling them into enormous, degraded heaps to be burned with napalm dropped from helicopters. A few people chained themselves to trees for half a day to protest.

The independent logger hadn't made much of a dent in the stands of beetle trees on my folks' property. You'd be surprised how many trees there are on forty acres of heavily timbered land. Even after two years, most of the dead pines were still standing. All the needles had come off by this time, and most of the bark. Loblolly pines, when they're crowded, tend to grow straight up toward the light like celery stalks, without much branching until they get up above the surrounding growth. Stripped of their needles and brown bark, they looked like silver spikes sticking in the sky. When the wind blew, they creaked and groaned as though they were swaying corpses lamenting their own death. Once in a while, when we'd have a storm, a few would come crashing down during the night.

Everyone was content to leave it this way—what else could they do, anyway? Most landowners felt lucky just to have the Forest Service off their backs, and my mother was glad not to have the logging truck churning up the soft hillside.

The dead pines fell, crushing other trees beneath them—

the young saplings of oak, sweet gum, and small-leaf maple, and the understory trees of dogwood, holly, and yaupon—and breaking big limbs off the older hardwoods. But gradually we all grew resigned to the ravaged woods. We went there less, not only because it was disheartening to see the wreck of what had been a hale loveliness, but because it was impossible to get through the tangle of deadfall.

"It's like a war zone," my mother said, and she was right. Like something had exploded and blown apart all the rhyme and reason of the woods. All the trails were blocked by broken limbs and trunks. All those trashy, opportunistic weeds like poke and mullein came crowding through every hole that was left in the crisscross of downed timber. This tangle was fine for birds and rabbits and snakes, but it made walking, or even clambering, almost impossible for people. We would walk down the lane, stand at the edge of the woods, and stare into them, barred from our own property by some secret plan of nature itself. We could see the new trees pushing through, even new pine seedlings. But my own grandchildren would be grown by the time these trees had made another forest like the one we had lost. And my parents knew they would probably not live to see it again as it had been before.

The practical problem of what to do about the fenceline and the barn on the edge of the woods remained, however. My parents tried to walk the line in November. They couldn't even make it halfway around the property. The fence that marked the boundaries between them and their neighbors was virtually gone. At other times this would not have been such a problem. But Mr. Locke, who owned the property to the north, had died the year before, and it was uncertain what his sons might do with it. A man who lived in Houston owned the property to the south. He kept cattle on it now, but developers had already been out in the area, trying to buy up blocks of land. He might decide to sell at any time.

Then there was the old hog barn down the lane threatened by the dead pines around it. Before the hurricane season began in August, my mother and father had gone down in the woods with their small chain saw and cut down a couple of trees that seemed likely to fall on the barn. It took them all day, and afterward the chain saw had to be taken in for repairs.

So when Slidell appeared in his battered Chevy pickup with a big shiny Poulan chain saw in the back, offering to clear away the beetle trees from the fenceline and the barn, my parents were glad to give him the job. One tree had already fallen during a storm and crashed into the roof of the lean-to on the back of the barn.

"I don't know where he's going to stay," my mother said. "I guess I should ask him to stay with us, but I know your father's not going to like that." Neither would she, it was clear. Slidell looked as though he had a lifetime of grime imbedded in his pores, and his face was a series of parenthetical wrinkles receding from his mouth and eyes like circles on the surface of a pond where a stone has been dropped. Just what the wrinkles bracketed, however, was a mystery. Slidell made a few vague references to picking oranges down in the lower Rio Grande valley and working as a short-order cook in San Antonio, but other than that he offered few clues to his background. It was obvious, though, that he wasn't the sort of person my parents usually had staying in their guest room. On the other hand, they couldn't in good conscience let him sleep in his truck in January, even though it looked as if that's what he'd been doing for some time.

But Slidell solved their problem for them. After they'd come to an agreement about cutting down the trees, he allowed as how he'd go down and visit my grandfather. He called him Uncle Ward. When he came back to get his chain saw after about an hour, Slidell announced that Uncle Ward had insisted that he stay with him while he was there.

"I'm not sure I like that arrangement," my mother told me that afternoon. "After all, we don't really know anything about him. He looks to me like somebody who drinks, and Daddy sure doesn't need that."

"Well, there doesn't seem much you can do about it now."

"I just hope he doesn't knock Daddy in the head and take that money he carries on him all the time. It's going to take more than a week for him to get this cutting done."

"What's the alternative?" I said. Slidell had already unloaded his belongings at my grandfather's. There seemed to be no going back now. At least he didn't own much, so he wouldn't be making my grandfather any offers like Ray Renfro had.

No one knows for sure what Slidell said to my grandfather on that first day. I suspect that it went something like this though. I think he introduced himself to my grandfather as "one of Archie's sons." There are a number of Archies in the family, starting with my grandfather's own Uncle Archie, the one who came to Texas first. Not wanting to appear as though he couldn't remember who this stranger was talking about, my grandfather would have simply said, "Sure, I remember you. Come on in. Have a seat."

And Slidell did.

Not only did he have a seat, but he had a bed, a bath, and however many meals a day my grandfather remembered to eat.

My grandfather couldn't have provided Slidell with a very varied menu. The only way he knew how to cook was to fry bacon, sausage, and eggs. And bake canned biscuits. Otherwise, he ate cereal, peanut butter, and bananas. My mother took him a pie or a cake at least once a week and she was constantly trying to get him to eat vegetables, which he left to rot in the refrigerator. But even considering the lack of variety, it was probably better food than Sly had seen in a long time.

I don't know when we started calling him Sly—probably not too long after he came. For although there was never any real evidence that he was up to no good with my grandfather, his general dinginess, his greasy, graying hair, and his constant, vacant parenthetical expression made all of us uneasy. All of us except my grandfather.

Yet even he called him Sly, it seemed like such an obvious

nickname. "Old Sly sure is something," he'd tell my mother when she came to gather up his dirty sheets and towels to wash—which she did almost daily now, as though she could get Sly clean just by providing him with enough fresh linen to rub up against.

One thing Sly was, it seemed, was a good listener. My grandfather was no longer interested in hearing any information about the outside world. He didn't understand what was going on there anyway. He didn't care who was running for office or who won ball games. He'd even given up buying the *National Enquirer* at Safeway. And since every sentence you said to him had to be repeated several times before he could get it right, the give-and-take that makes up an ordinary conversation was lost.

On the other hand, he reeled off stories, most often only fragments now with frequent reprises, from his dwindling stock of tales, some actual, some imaginary, most a mixture. Any remark made by the other party, any mention of a place or an occasion, only worked as a trigger for recounting his own experience. We had grown used to scanning the latest *National Geographic* while he rambled on, paying just enough attention to pick up any new deviation in his story that might be a clue to his present mental or emotional condition.

But Sly was different. He sat on the edge of the chair on the other side of the lamp, his shoulders angled slightly toward the old man, and nodded his head every now and then, never taking his eyes off my grandfather's face, except to suddenly throw himself back in the chair in a move meant to express his surprise and astonishment.

Yet he never voluntarily said anything to us about my grandfather or his declining faculties. In another person we might have seen this as a mark of respect for the old man despite his failing powers, or at least as cautiousness about offending any of the family by treating his condition too flippantly.

My mother, still suspicious, tried to draw him out. "I hope Dad's not too much of a bother to you, Slidell," she said one morning as he was oiling up his chain saw in the garage. A norther had blown in the night before.

"No ma'am. Me and him, we get along just fine."

"I know those stories of his get awful old after a while though."

"Oh, I enjoy hearing about what Uncle Ward's been up to all his life. I figure we're just making up for lost time."

"Well. I wouldn't take some of those stories too seriously. Especially those about his trips around the world. He just imagines he's been some of those places—Japan and China and South America. I guess you'd recognize that though. You've probably done quite a lot of traveling yourself."

The parentheses around Sly's mouth inched out a space as he smiled wryly. "I've been around a right smart," was all he said. There didn't seem to be any way she could get more information about his origins out of him unless she quizzed him directly. And, after all, as her own grandfather had said, when he came to Texas, that wasn't a question you asked a man.

Neither she nor my father had anything to complain about when it came to Slidell's work. He was out in the woods every morning as soon as it was light, the chain saw's undulating, rachety roar coming hoarsely through the trees. I could even hear it faintly from my house on the hill. The noise was so steady throughout the day that it almost lulled one's senses. After a while we noticed it only when he turned the chain saw off and the silence, solid and silvery, descended again.

Nor did he bother my folks by hanging around the house, as they had at first feared might turn out to be the case. He went to the woods in the morning, worked steadily till noon, went back up to my grandfather's house for lunch, stayed about an hour and a half, and returned again to the woods to work till sundown—or what would have been sundown if the sun had come out. That January was particularly gray. The sun came out only a couple of times, once for the Oilers' play-off game and again for the Super Bowl. Not that Sly showed any interest in either. On weekends he disappeared—we supposed into town.

At first my folks worried that he might not show up again to finish the job. My father insisted on paying him at the end of each week, although my mother was afraid he might take off with the first cash he got in his hands. But on Monday mornings he was always hard at it again.

When he began, despite his appearance, to prove himself reliable, they started in worrying about his being a burden to my grandfather. He might well be some long-lost great-nephew, but he still had to eat three meals a day. Not that the old man couldn't afford to feed him; my mother routinely had to throw out spoiled food from his refrigerator because he always bought far more than he ever ate.

Still, she fretted. "It takes a good bit to feed a man working as hard as Slidell does," she said. "I'd be glad to feed him up here at the house. We're the ones that *ought* to be feeding him. After all, he's working for us. And we're not paying him all that much. Besides, he has to be getting tired of eggs and bacon all the time."

But when she asked him if he wouldn't like to eat with them, Sly just shook his head and pulled the parentheses up over his eyebrows. "No'm. I'll just stick with where I am. Looks like Uncle Ward don't mind having me. He seems glad of a little company." He looked up at her narrowly. "And I intend to pay him for my vittles when I finish up here. I'm keeping account."

"Oh heavens, that's not what I meant at all," she said. "Don't misunderstand me. You're earning ever bit of what we're able to pay you, and more. That's why I thought I could cook a little better for you, or at least something different. You must get tired of the same old thing day after day."

"No'm," he said again and grinned. "Uncle Ward and me're getting along just fine." And something about that remark made her more uneasy than ever.

"We do try to get him to eat up here as often as possible," she went on. "But he almost always says he's just finished eating."

"Yes'm. But now that I'm there with him, he sort of enjoys the company, you know. So I feel like I ought to keep it up. You know what I mean?"

She just wished he wouldn't keep calling her "ma'am."

She wasn't that much older than he was, anyway. That afternoon she made up a big pot of chili, took it down to my grandfather's house, and left it on the stove. Three days later she had to throw it out. It hadn't been touched.

However worrisome my parents found Slidell's presence, my grandfather was delighted with his new guest. For the first few days he couldn't remember that Sly had moved in, and he kept stumbling over the paper sack Sly kept his few belongings in and wondering whose coat it was hanging on the hat tree by the door. But as soon as the routine that Slidell established began to wear a groove in his memory, my grandfather started to count on his appearing at noon for lunch and again when the sun began to go down. My folks could see his lamp burning a little longer than usual in the evenings, and when they drove by, they could see the figure of Sly leaning on his elbow toward my grandfather, who was punctuating the air with his crooked forefinger as he told one of his stories.

"I don't like it," my mother said. "It's unnatural. He can't possibly like eating like that. Or sitting there night after night listening to Daddy's stories. I just know he must be after something."

"Well, what do you think we should do about it?" my father replied. "Do you want me to get rid of him?"

"How would you do that? He's doing a good job, isn't he?"

"So far as I can tell."

"Have you been down to look at the fenceline?"

"A couple of times already. Looks to me like he's doing okay. I don't want the guy to get the idea we're looking over his shoulder."

"How much more does he have to go?"

"He's already onto the east side. If he keeps up like he's been going, it shouldn't take too much longer. Maybe three or four days."

She crossed her arms in front of her and turned away. "Well, I guess it'll be all right. But I sure feel uneasy about it. I wish he was gone already. I can't help feeling there's something going on down there with Daddy."

My father, on the other hand, felt relieved. To tell the truth, he didn't know how in the world Sly was managing it; the man was obviously well past his prime, yet he worked like a twenty-year-old, a robust one at that. My father wanted very badly for Sly to finish clearing the fenceline. There wasn't any telling when he and my mother would be able to get the job done otherwise. So although he felt uneasy with the situation too, he let it go for the time being. Both he and my mother figured that the job would soon be done and Sly would be on his way. They had even already agreed that, when he finished, they would give him a fifty-dollar bonus.

By this time I was curious about Sly myself. I had been surprised when my folks hired him. I was sure that if he hadn't claimed to be a relative, they never would have. He simply wasn't the kind of person they were used to dealing with. But I found it even more surprising that my grandfather had taken such a shine to him. Since Sly had arrived on the scene, I had seen my grandfather briefly only a couple of times. The first time, he was in the truck when my father stopped by to bring the mail. When I asked him about his new boarder, he only looked at me in a puzzled way. But the next time, when I stopped by on my way to my folks' house, he met me at the door, smiling and eager. When he saw it was only me, he sat down again.

"I thought you was Sly," he said.

"You two getting along okay?" I asked.

"Good as two old bachelors can make it," he said. He didn't seem to be very interested in talking that day, so I went on about my business.

The next afternoon I had free, however, I went to see him for a longer visit, figuring Sly would still be down in the woods. My grandfather was out in his front yard, looking at his straggling rosebushes. He has about five, and he never prunes them, though my mother often takes her snippers to them. He lets the canes keep growing as long as they will.

"How're they doing?" I asked as I came up.

"No buds yet," he said.

"It's only January," I said. "There never are any buds this time of year. You'll have to wait a while."

He looked at me closely. "Not this year," he said. "This year's different."

I shrugged. What do you say to a man who's been to China and Tierra del Fuego?

We went inside, and I noticed that, even though he looked like a drying leaf, flimsy and curling inward on itself, when he maneuvered up the steps ahead of me he wasn't dragging his feet across the floor with his old man's unsteady shuffle, but was lifting them a little higher and stepping a bit more smartly. I sat down in the listener's chair, but instead of collapsing into his old Naugahyde throne, he stood with his back to the space heater, warming himself.

"So you and Slidell are getting along okay, are you?"

"Pretty tol'able well, daughter." It was hard for him to keep the eagerness out of his voice, but at the same time it was obvious he didn't care to expand on the reasons for his enthusiasm. He was keeping a secret.

"Good. I'm glad you've got somebody to keep you company."

He sat down in his chair without making any comment.

"I guess he doesn't mind your cooking, either," I said. I wasn't going to be put off so easily.

"I 'spect not." But now a frown passed over his face. "Leastwise he never says nothing about it. On the other hand, he sure don't eat much."

"Working as hard as he does every day, and he doesn't eat much?"

He looked over at me, suddenly startled. "Oh, I don't know," he said quickly, trying to cover up. "I don't pay much attention to another man's appetite. I reckon that's his own lookout."

"Does he have any family?" I asked next. "Has he ever said anything about a wife or children?"

"Not to the best of my recollection," my grandfather replied. "Of course, I don't ask nobody about nothing they don't volunteer on their own." And he looked at me pointedly.

"Well, he sure is a curious character," I said. "Have you got him to play checkers with you yet?"

"No. No, don't seem like he's interested in playing no games."

What I wanted to ask next was what the two of them did, sitting around here in the winter evenings, besides going over all my grandfather's old tales of the war and the Texas riverbottoms. But there are some questions you can never ask, no matter how curious you are, because to ask them would mean you would never find out the answer. It would be like saying outright, "What does he see in an old man like you? What's he got up his sleeve?"

I sat there silent for a while, trying to come up with another way of approaching the subject and looking around the familiar bare-floored room with the two old sofas, the blank television set, and the homemade coffee table with the aqua Formica top holding family pictures and a bowl of Christmas nuts, hoping to see if Sly had left any personal possession, any piece of clothing or book or belonging that might give some clue to the man.

My grandfather spoke again, as though unable to contain his excitement. "That Sly. He's some character."

"Does he like fishing?" I asked. I couldn't get the specter of Renfro out of my mind.

"Fishing? I don't recall him ever saying if *he* liked it or not. But he sure understands the other fella a-liking it."

"He doesn't have a cabin down on the river, does he?"

"Sly?" my grandfather said innocently, not catching the allusion. "I don't reckon Sly has much of anything. But he says he knows some good places to go."

"Oh?" He was talking eagerly, and I didn't want to make him balk now by asking too many questions.

"He's been around, that Sly. Why, he even knows some of the same folks I been a-knowing all my life."

"Is that so?" I said cautiously.

"You betcha. And here I thought ever body'd forgotten them."

"I'll be."

"Why, he even knows where. . ." He stopped suddenly, sighed, and clasped his hands together. "Hmm," he said, smiling to himself. "Yessir. Old Sly." He looked over at me again, as though he were weighing something in his mind.

"Just how old do you reckon old Sly is?" I said.

"What?" The expression on his face melted away. "What'd you say?"

"Just how old is Sly?"

"How would I know?" he answered shortly. "I don't go around asking folks what I figure ain't none of my business."

We didn't say much more after that as we sat by the fire, and I remember thinking about the difference two years had made. Now I knew all the stories he'd been able to tell; some of them he didn't remember himself anymore. I'd done what I could to salvage something of him, something from his past. But most of it no one would ever know. He was like the forest, ravaged and full of waste, the pathways to his long life clogged with the tangled debris of his own brain. But there was no way to clear the forest of his mind now. Only a cauterizing fire could do that.

After a while I got up to leave, figuring Sly might be coming in soon. For some reason I had an aversion to talking to the man himself. It wasn't his general greasiness or his peculiarly unsuitable clothes that bothered me so much as it was his air of knowing exactly what he was up to, which included his counting on the fact that you would never ask him about it directly. He must have known that neither I nor my parents were too happy about his staying there with my grandfather, but he went ahead with his work and his plans as though what we thought made no difference at all to him. There was something about Sly, ragtag-bobtail vagabond that he was, that showed he knew we couldn't touch him.

"Well, good-bye, Pawpaw," I said when I left, and bent

over his chair to kiss his pink skull. "You be careful now. It's supposed to come a hard freeze tonight. Make sure you've got plenty of covers on your bed." Somehow I felt reluctant to leave him there to that unknown quantity.

He grinned up at me, looking expectant again. "Don't you be worrying about me, daughter. It's you that's got to face that world out there." I heard him chuckling to himself as I closed the door.

———————

THAT WAS the way I left him. Laughing to himself over some secret scheme. I don't mind that, not even after all that happened later. If he was keeping a secret from the rest of us, I guess he's got it still.

CASKET PRICE LIST

THE PRICES ARE EFFECTIVE AS OF AUGUST 20, 1988, BUT ARE
SUBJECT TO CHANGE WITHOUT NOTICE.

To assist you in identifying a casket, we have assigned a numerical symbol to each casket. A corresponding numerical symbol has been affixed to the upper left-hand corner of the casket price card which is inside or attached to the casket.

1. Protective, Masterpiece, 48 oz. Bronze, Silver	$8691.00
2. Protective, Winchester, 32 oz. Bronze, Brushed Natural	$4698.00
3. Non-Protective, Executive, Hardwood, Walnut	$3891.00
4. Protective, Lincoln, Copper, Painted Bronze	$2991.00
5. Protective, Lincoln, Copper, Painted Blue	$2991.00
6. Protective, Lincoln, Copper, Painted White	$2991.00
7. Protective, Tea Rose, Stainless Steel, Tea Rose	$2791.00
8. Protective, Lancaster, 18 GA., Venetian Bronze	$2594.00
9. Protective, Winthrop, 18 GA., Gunmetal	$2394.00
10. Protective, Electra, 18 GA., Heather	$2298.00
11. Non-Protective, Meadowland, Pine 854, Natural	$2298.00
12. Protective, Courtland, 20 GA., Brown	$1488.00
13. Non-Protective, Barron, 20 GA., Green	$1198.00
14. Non-Protective, #750, Cloth 6/3, Silver	$893.00
15. Non-Protective, #100, Cloth Flat Top, Gray	$599.00

Rental Caskets: Units 3 through 14 one-half retail price

Alternative Containers:

1. Cardboard Container	$100.00
2. Air Trays	$75.00
3. Disaster Pouch	$85.00
4. Inner Sealer (Ziegler Case)	$299.00
5. Sealed in Tin Liner (Lead Sealed, Medaris Sheet Metal)	$750.00

THE DESCRIPTIONS "PROTECTIVE" AND "NON-PROTECTIVE" ARE THE MAN-UFACTURERS'. ALTHOUGH CERTAIN CASKETS OFFERED FOR SALE BY THE FUNERAL ESTABLISHMENT MAY BE OF BETTER QUALITY CONSTRUCTION AND COMPRISED OF MORE DURABLE MATERIALS THAN OTHERS, NEITHER THIS FUNERAL ESTABLISHMENT NOR ANY OF ITS EMPLOYEES REPRESENTS OR IM-PLIES THAT ANY CASKET WILL BE AIR TIGHT OR WATER TIGHT OR WILL PROVIDE LONG-TERM PRESERVATION OF HUMAN REMAINS.

The Judgment

We who knew our fathers
in everything, in nothing.

They perish. They cannot be brought back.
The secret worlds are not regenerated.

And everytime again and again
I make my lament against destruction.

—Yevgeny Yevtushenko

IT WASN'T the last time I saw him, of course. The last time was in the Westerfield Funeral Home, laid out in the satin-lined coffin paid for by the money from the Guardian Plan II.

He looked good. Not natural, maybe, the standard compliment people in my family always pay corpses. After all, he had on a suit. But my mother had insisted on the bolo tie he usually wore instead of the silk one someone bought for the occasion. The mortician had toned down the color of his hawk-like nose. In fact, there seemed to be a sort of silvery dusting of powder all over him, as though a spidery membrane were separating him from us. His hands were folded across his stomach, the hand with the crooked forefinger on top. After everyone had filed by the casket, the lid was closed, and that was the last any of us saw of him.

Which was more than we saw of Slidell, though the authorities searched for him in five states.

The whole experience nearly put my mother in the grave herself. The morning after my last visit with my grandfather, a Saturday, she had gone down to my grandfather's house to strip the beds again. Slidell's pickup was gone from the driveway, but she figured he had gone into town for the weekend. Then she discovered that the front door was locked, and she couldn't see a light in any of the rooms. She knocked at both the front and the back doors, but no one came.

She had to go back to her house to get the key to let herself in. She said that as she was going across the field which separates the two houses, she was already beginning to feel uneasy. She knew that either my grandfather had gone off with Sly to town—something he hadn't done before—or the "something" she was always worrying about had at last happened. She wasn't too sure, even then, which would have been worse.

When she let herself in by the kitchen door, she found everything tidier than usual. All the dishes had been washed and put up out of the drainer. There was no iron skillet sitting on the stove full of leftover bacon grease, no plate of cold biscuits left on the table. The countertops had all been wiped clean and the chairs pushed in at the table. In her father's bedroom the bed was neatly made, and all the clothes normally left draped over the chair were put away. Even the sink in the bathroom had been recently scrubbed and the towels were hanging straight.

All this made her feel even more uneasy, but it wasn't until she checked in the living room that she was sure something was wrong. The fire in the space heater was burning, and the room was warm, as though my grandfather had just walked out the door a moment before. My grandfather never left the house with the fire burning. It was the one thing he never forgot.

My mother sat down gingerly on the edge of his chair and

put her hand to her throat. She told herself there was probably some perfectly reasonable explanation for all this. But her fear was so sudden and so profound that her knees went weak and she couldn't force a sound from her throat. Her eyes darted about the room, looking for something, anything, a clue as to where he had gone, what had happened.

There was nothing. Everything looked the same as it always did. She saw the same magazines and catalogues and Masonic books stacked on the coffee table and next to his chair. The same bowl and nuts with the nutcracker. A box of candy and another of raisins. An old sheet of peel-off corn plasters. Two harmonicas. The family pictures. Nothing appeared to have been touched. If anything, this room, like the others, was neater than usual. The wastebasket my grandfather kept beside his chair had just been emptied. There wasn't even much dust.

She got up, went out the front door and down the porch steps, then walked all around the house twice. Nothing looked disturbed. The garbage can by the kitchen corner of the house was also empty. She checked the gauge on the propane tank. It was full. The lock on the toolshed was secure and rusty. She walked around to the front of the house again. The only thing that was any different was that a bud on my grandfather's white rosebush had opened that morning.

She went back inside and phoned for my father to come down. Then she called me.

"You haven't seen your grandfather, have you?" she said.

"Why would I have seen him? Isn't he there?"

"No. I can't find him anywhere. And that — man — is gone too."

"Man?" I repeated. "You mean Slidell?"

"Yes. I guess he's taken Daddy off somewhere." And now, for the first time, she started to cry.

"Now just calm down, Mother. You don't know what's happened. Don't go jumping to any conclusions."

"Well, I'm going to send your daddy out to look for them. And if he can't find them, I'm going to call the sheriff."

"Tell him to stop here and pick me up and I'll go with him."

In a few minutes my father's pickup came creeping up the red clay road. "What were you doing?" I asked him as I crawled in beside him. "Searching the bushes?" I was trying to make light of their fear, for my own sake as much as theirs.

"You never know," he said. "Stranger things have happened. I never did trust that man. I told your mother that from the start." His voice was shaking.

I didn't ask him stranger things than what. Or just what it was they thought had happened. It was obvious they were expecting the worst.

———

IT WASN'T, of course, the worst that happened. (I wonder what would have been the worst, or if the worst can ever happen, since you can always imagine something more terrible than what actually does happen.) But when the sheriff finally found my grandfather, it was bad enough.

There's a short-line railroad up in Anderson County that runs the thirteen miles between Palestine and Rusk. It's part of a state park and is operated as a historic monument of sorts, carrying tourists who want to see what riding a turn-of-the-century train is like. You have to make reservations ahead of time in the summer, but during the winter months the train doesn't run at all because it has open passenger cars. It has a steam engine like my grandfather used to work on when he was a young man, first right there in Palestine and later out in Amarillo, where my grandmother died. Maybe that's what explains why he and Sly went there, of all places.

In the winter a park attendant comes around to check the premises every morning, and that's how my grandfather was found, asleep on a bench in front of the refurbished gingerbread depot, as if he were waiting for a train. Slidell's old truck was parked in the lot, the keys still in it. But his paper sack with his belongings, whatever they might have been, and his chain saw were gone.

My grandfather was suffering from exposure, having spent at least one night out in the cold and possibly two. But he hadn't been abused or beaten up, and he still had seven hundred dollars in his pocket. It reminded me of Tolstoy, how he'd run away from home at the last, away from his wife and children, who were feuding over him, an old, decrepit man half out of his head, and how he'd died there at the train siding, refusing to see members of his family.

Of course, they took my grandfather right to the hospital in Palestine, but he never really woke up fully. His pulse had been weak when they found him, and it didn't get any stronger. His chest, which had been a little congested about a week before he disappeared, now rattled with his shallow breathing. It had been very cold the night before they found him, down in the twenties. There was no evidence of, as they say, foul play. And legally, of course, there was nothing to keep Sly from taking my grandfather off with him if my grandfather wanted to go—which, of course, he had no doubt been all too willing to do. Because of that, and also because all the money was still in my grandfather's pocket, the sheriff wasn't much interested in trying to track Sly down, although he sent out a bulletin over the police computer-network to the surrounding states. And my mother's immediate concern, of course, was not Slidell but her father.

"Don't let them put him on any life-support systems, Esther, you hear?" Bess had said when my mother called her from the hospital. "Not even oxygen. This could drag on forever that way. And him not even wake up again. You just stay right there with him so if he does wake up he'll see someone familiar. And make sure they keep him comfortable. I ought to be there in three or four hours. I'm leaving now."

He was in intensive care at the little hospital in Palestine, the city where he had grown up, in too delicate a condition to be moved. The young doctor who explained this to my mother looked at her strangely, as though he couldn't understand how the old man had come to be in this shape.

"You see, we had these pine trees," she began. By the time she got to Slidell showing up with his chain saw, the doctor broke in.

"That's not important now," he said. "We'll just have to see if he has enough strength left to snap back. You ought to prepare yourselves for the fact that that might not be the case. Two nights out in the cold. Hypothermia. All that on top of this congestion he already had in the lungs." And he disappeared down the hall.

I slipped into the cubicle where they had my grandfather and stood beside my mother. By then, after they'd cleaned him up, he didn't look much worse than usual. I'm glad she didn't have to see him as he must have been when they brought him in. Now he was sleeping, but his breathing was shallow. She took his hand and held it for a long time. After a while his eyelids fluttered. I went around and stood on the other side of his bed.

"Dad?" she said. "It's me, Esther."

He sighed and closed his eyes again.

She went and stood by the window for a few minutes. I was watching her to see how she was holding up, but after a while I looked back at my grandfather. His eyes were wide open, and he was smiling up at the ceiling. His hand moved on the blanket.

"May," he said suddenly. "He told me May would be. . . They want music. They want me to play . . ." He closed his eyes again.

My mother had come quickly to the bedside as soon as she heard him stir. She took his hand again. "Dad?"

His eyes fluttered open again. "I'm going," he said. "I'm a-going with him. You can't stop me."

―――――

"IT WAS MURDER," Sally said, out in the hospital hall. We had been there all day, my folks and I. She had just arrived, about an hour too late. My mother had finished calling all the rest of her brothers and sisters except Bess, who was already on her way.

"You don't mean it," Ward had said. "Just like that? He just took off without telling anybody? Well, I'll be damned."

There had been a long pause on the other end of the line when she had called Rachel. "I'll let Parker know," she finally said. "He can drive us up to Springfield, and we can get a plane from there. You get some rest now, sister."

It had taken some doing to find Irene. The last anybody knew, she had been living with her husband's daughter-in-law and working at a country club outside of Atlanta. In fact, it was at the club that my mother was finally able to reach her. My father and I watched her face anxiously until we saw her mouth the words "She's sober" with her hand over the mouthpiece.

"Irene, I have some bad news for you, honey," she said. "It's Dad." And her voice broke. It was complicated, getting all the details straight so that Irene could understand what had happened.

"Well, how come?" she kept saying. "What did he do that for? You mean you just let him go off like that?" By the time my mother put down the phone, she was shaking. She had told Irene she'd wire her the money to fly home for the funeral.

That was about the time Sally got there.

"Well, no, it's not exactly murder," I said.

"Criminal, then," she said, snapping her black patent handbag shut with a sharp click. "I'm going to talk to the sheriff about this. Taking an old man off like that against his will. There's got to be some kind of law against that."

My mother spoke up. "But we don't even know that it was against his will. For all we know, he may have been quite happy to go. In fact, I wouldn't be at all surprised. That man could have promised him—who knows what all—and Daddy would have gone off just like a little child."

"That's just it," Sally said. "It was just like enticing a child away from home. Criminal."

I, on the other hand, always thought we owed a lot to

Sly. For one thing, he provided everyone with a welcome distraction from the fact of their father's death. They went over and over the details of the story of his disappearance, inventing endless possibilities for what might have happened. Sam speculated that Slidell was probably involved in a drug ring. Irene, however, was of the opinion that Sly must have intended to hold their daddy for ransom. She said if we'd only search the house thoroughly, we'd probably find a ransom note. Ward and Bess got out a map and traced possible escape routes Sly could have taken. Sally called her lawyer to ask about various charges they might be able to bring against Sly.

As I say, he was never found anyway, so it all came to nothing in the end, but it gave everyone a lot to talk about at the funeral so that they didn't have to go through the spiritual autopsy my family is prone to. A man like my grandfather provides plenty of material for that kind of analysis, of course. His life was such a tantalizing tangle, of virtue and vice, circumstance and motive, spiritual perspicacity and negligence, that I don't see how they would have ever teased all his strands apart to everyone's mutual satisfaction. Some would have wanted to emphasize his good points, while others would have felt obliged to mention his failings. My mother and Bess would have insisted on the theological validity of his baptism and held out against the notion of his falling from grace. The skeptics would have made light of the idea that a little bit of murky river-water could wash away the stains from a soul as manifestly stubborn as his was.

I don't know why we feel the need to do this kind of postmortem judgment, but we do. It's hard, on the one hand, to keep from veering off toward sentimentality. There's the natural tendency to want to say only good things about the dead. But pretty soon, especially with someone like my grandfather, you realize you've gotten beyond the bounds of reality. So you back up and try to balance the scale with a few tough, hard, cold facts. But then you remember what he was up against, the adversity you're not sure you could have handled any better, if as well. So you begin to back off again. And not always because you're afraid of being unfair. Sometimes it's because you can almost hear echoes reaching you from some future funeral parlor where people are sitting around assessing your own final worth. And suddenly you have an urge to be more generous. And so it goes: you veer back and forth, trying to trace at least the general outline of a life, to weigh the worth of someone in the cosmic scheme of things. And always, in every case, it ends up sounding banal and demeaning.

After three days, I believe his children were almost ready to thank Slidell for saving them from all that. Because of him, they could afford to be a little tenderer of one another's feelings than they might have been otherwise. They could be content with saying things like,

"Well, at least he didn't suffer."

"Not much, anyway."

"And he was happy, I guess."

"Yes. He seems to have died happy."

———

YESTERDAY, after they'd all left, I went out to the woods, determined to penetrate them at least as far as Mr. Locke's pond. I wore an old jacket and boots for scrabbling over the fallen trees and through the underbrush. I often find myself imagining how the woods must have looked to the Caddo Indians who once lived here. They came, some historians speculate, from the Yucatán peninsula down in Mexico, sailing straight north across the Gulf. When they got here, they continued the Aztec and Incan tradition of making ceremonial pyramids that faced east. The piney woods being short on stones, however, they built their pyramids out of dirt and faced them with logs. Eventually, like all living things in this climate, the logs rotted, and the pyramids slumped into rounded mounds.

The Caddos were primarily an agricultural people, preferring farming to fighting. They stayed off the treeless plains, the habitat of the buffalo, to avoid upsetting Apache hunters. They traded with the Pueblos further west for cotton cloth, and when the French and Spanish arrived on the scene, they were eager to trade with them too. Relations between the Caddos and the Europeans were always surprisingly good, but then no one could have foreseen the effect of one foreign import—disease. By 1800 the Caddo Indians were all but extinct, wiped out by smallpox, measles, and other European microbes.

I was lucky. Mr. Locke's son had been down with his chain saw and cleared away some of the worst deadfall tangles. I made it to the pond, my jeans covered with beggar-lice seedpods, but with only a few scratches from the brambles. The pond was still, its surface that lovely color between copper and silver. I sat down on a bare log, stripped of its bark by the beetles two years ago and itself silvered from more than one season of rain and wind.

I thought about the Caddos and how they were shaped by the land too. I wondered how many Caddo bones I'd been walking over. I tried to look through the understory of trees, the holly and the dogwood and the myrtle, the same way they did, maybe trying to spot a squirrel to shoot or huckleberries to strip from the low branches. I thought about their lives and what they have meant, what they mean, for the rest of us. What does any life—obscure, unrecorded, gone forever—mean? How can it mean, if it goes unrecorded? Do all those lives of the Caddos, lives of voiceless pagans, mean only en masse, only as a lump in the generalized outline of history?

The Caddo whose eyes I was trying to see through surely must have felt his life as keenly as I do mine, must have been pricked by the sudden shimmer of light in the leaves, the sharp winter scents of fallow, upturned earth, must have yearned after life the way I do, the way my grandfather did. In their central temple the high priest kept an eternal flame burning, a flame from which all other temple fires of the tribes had to be lit. They knew death was coming; they too feared eternal extinction.

I imagined my own bones lying six feet under the layers of sand, loam, and clay. In two hundred years, who knows what foreign feet may be walking over my own head? They will never have heard of me, and at best will know no more of my life than a few broad outlines of my times, the way I know the Caddos, the way the world, even now, knows my grandfather. Why then, I wonder, should there be something so indescribably sweet to us about our own lives, when they go unremarked by anyone other than a few friends and family members? We cast our minds back over our span of years, trying to discern patterns, lingering over certain episodes, fingering old artifacts of ourselves, wondering what they mean.

———————

ALL MY GRANDFATHER'S children have left again. Except, of course, my mother. Somehow I don't feel like things will be much different here. Not yet. I'll still expect him to be sitting over there in his house, huddled up by the heater, dreaming his past. But gradually that will wear off, and I'll get used to the house being empty. I'll help my mother go through all his belongings, taking what clothes are still usable down to the Good Shepherd Mission, divvying up his personal effects—his pocketknife, his big round pocketwatch, his pictures and Masonic regalia—among whichever of his children might want them.

There'll be some hassles over what money he left and the acre of land with a house on it that nobody wants. But eventually the younger ones will have their way, and my mother and Bess, the two oldest, will acquiesce in whatever the rest want. My father won't be pleased.

The pine saplings have already started growing up on that acre where my grandfather once grew cotton and forty years later built a house. They'll get taller and taller, and after a while they'll block the view from my folks' house. Birds and snakes and deer will move back in, though my mother will try to keep the brush cleared out around the rosebushes and the peach trees he planted.

We'll start to talk about him again without the funereal wreaths of sentiment scrolling out of our mouths. My daughters will remember him the way I remember people who disappeared over the brow of the hill just as I was coming up the slope—as someone they knew, but not well. They'll remember him as he was after he was old. And their children will remember him not at all. He will forever be to them a mythic figure, just like his father, Silas, riding into Texas from Mississippi, is to me. Or like the Caddo Indians.

But I'll remember him, as much of him as I knew, which was far from all. In order to remind myself that he was real, all of him, all the long dim years, and that reality neither stops nor begins with me but stretches out on either side of now.